THE COST OF FREEDOM

THE

COST

OF

FREEDOM

A New Look at Capitalism

HENRY C. WALLICH

Member President's Council of Economic Advisers
Professor of Economics, Yale University, on leave

GREENWOOD PRESS, PUBLISHERS
WESTPORT, CONNECTICUT

Library of Congress Cataloging in Publication Data

Wallich, Henry Christopher, 1914-
   The cost of freedom.

   Reprint of the ed. published by Harper, New York.
   Includes bibliographical references and index.
   1. Capitalism. 2. Economic policy. 3. Liberty.
I. Title.
[HD82.W25 1979]   330.12'2   78-27775
ISBN 0-313-20935-9

Published in 1960 by Harper & Brothers, Publishers, New York

Reprinted with the permission of Harper & Row, Publishers, Inc.

Reprinted in 1979 by Greenwood Press, Inc.
51 Riverside Avenue, Westport, CT 06880

Printed in the United States of America

10 9 8 7 6 5 4 3 2 1

To M. I. W.

CONTENTS

PREFACE

The decision to write this book reflects a concern of many years standing with the intellectual underpinnings of a modern economic conservatism. This is a point of view that has found expression more effectively perhaps in action than in writing. In the face of many eloquent and persuasive statements from the liberal wing, I hope to contribute to the constructive case that can be made on the other side.

If that case is to be made effectively, it must take its departure from an honest reexamination of old beliefs. Change is the price of progress; what matters is that change possess continuity. From the point of view of this book, there is good to be found in the teachings of both Adam Smith and John Maynard Keynes.

The message that the book carries can be put in simplest terms. Our free economy has been highly successful. To obtain its full benefits, we must accept the need for certain efforts and sacrifices. We must maintain strong incentives and vigorous competition, and must be prepared to live with some of the consequences that these arrangements imply. We must accept some degree of economic inequality, which incentives and competition are bound to create. And while we can expect a good rate of economic growth, we must be prepared to forego the extra gain that forced draft methods might yield because they would not be compatible with freedom in peace-time. The ultimate value of a free economy is not production, but freedom, and freedom comes not at a profit, but at a cost.

In formulating these propositions, I have drawn upon many ideas that are common property, though I hope not entirely commonplace. Some of them found a preliminary expression in an article that I published in the *Yale Review* in the Fall of 1956, and I have elaborated upon them here. I have had the generous help of many friends, colleagues, and other good counselors, in discussions extending in some instances over many years. To all of them I am glad to acknowledge a lasting debt. Needless to say, the responsibility for a man's views can never be anyone's but his own.

A tour of duty in Washington does not provide as many free evenings and Sundays for outside writing as I might have wished. But if this condition is in part accountable for some of the book's shortcomings, it also has imposed the virtue of brevity. More than anything, it has conferred the privilege of a perspective from the center, and the stimulation of a highly charged atmosphere.

H. C. W.

Washington, D.C.
May, 1960

I

THE NEED FOR A NEW LOOK

THIS book undertakes to reexamine some of the principles upon which our economic system is built. It is part of the strength of America that on basic principles we have traditionally enjoyed a high degree of consensus. No one in America questions democracy and personal freedom. Few would question private property and private enterprise. Free markets, free competition, and the limited role of government are generally accepted. On matters of this order we stand united, and our debates, which are many, start from this infra-structure of consensus.

The basic consensus has gained strength, in the years after World War II, from the satisfactory functioning of the economy. Today, fifteen years after World War II, we look upon a scene very different from that which confronted the nation at an equal distance from World War I. In terms of this comparison, 1960 is the equivalent of 1933. In 1933, many millions had lost their jobs, savings had been wiped out, the nation's income cut to levels of many years ago. In bitterness and doubt, theories of permanent stagnation were beginning to take shape. Today, we can look back upon a postwar period in which major depressions have been avoided, at the same time that growing numbers of people have enjoyed rapidly rising standards of living, security, and leisure. Fear of stagnation has given way to expectation of permanent growth. Our recent experience has been a vindication of the basic features of our economy.

In Western Europe, the renaissance of capitalism has been even more dramatic. Carried forward by high rates of growth, the European economies have swept away the debris of the war. Mass production and mass consumption are transforming the life of the Old World. Faced with this refutation of their doctrines, the old time socialist parties of Britain and Germany are beginning to jettison socialism. Western Europe today is giving the world an object lesson in the principles of a free economy.

The Challenge to Capitalism

YET at this time when capitalism is performing better perhaps than ever before, it is also being challenged more deeply than ever before. The challenge comes from a rival system that asserts powers of growth faster than ours, and makes no bones about its intention to bury us if it can. This system draws single-minded strength from a philosophy held with religious intensity and oriented with total ruthlessness toward its goal. Its recent successes, however one-sided, have demonstrated the power behind the threat. In the face of the Russian example, the uses of capitalism are being challenged also by some of the underdeveloped countries of the world. Confronted today with the need to make up for lost time, they wonder whether to travel the road of a free economy, or whether they can proceed more quickly by some other route.

Our principles, as well as our performance, are being weighed as they have never been weighed before.

The external challenges, in turn, have generated doubt at home. Concern lest the economy fail to respond adequately has produced a spate of proposals, not so much to change the basic character of the economy, but to modify its operation. Most of the proposals for raising our rate of growth by sharply stepping up public expenditures—at the cost, possibly, of continuing inflation—do not seem deliberately to call in question the basic character of a free economy. Their authors, whether from sympathy for the existing system or indifference, seem prepared to work within the existing mold. The consensus on fundamentals appears to remain intact. Nevertheless, proposals of this kind come dangerously close to demands for a forced draft economy. If administered for any length of time, they might very well lead to basic changes in the economy, intended or not. Progress is never so rapid as when it leads downhill.

These challenges pose momentous issues for a free economy. They require a determined reexamination of its basic principles. We must, first of all, remind ourselves why we believe in a free economy. Are our chief grounds that we believe it to be the most productive? Or do we prefer it because it helps safeguard personal freedom? Or, finally, is preference for free enterprise perhaps just a rationalization of personal advantage? If we understand our reasons and motives more clearly, we shall have a better view of the choices before us. We shall see in better perspective the risk and cost of alternative courses of action. And from such materials we can construct a stronger case and project a more persuasive image to present to sceptics at home and abroad. These must be the principal objectives of reexamination.

People who consider themselves practical may object that our principles are manifest in our action, and that there is no need for theorizing. They may prefer profitable investment in the market to unprofitable speculation in economic doctrine. Yet we are not necessarily being "practical" if, in Tawney's words, we take things as they are and leave them as they were. Reexamination, to be sure, is always postponable, the process rather painful, the results often discomforting. The fact remains that there is no substitute for live ideas. Even great truths are not imperishable. The truths of yesterday have a habit of becoming the slogans of today. To stay alive, truth and conviction need to be nourished by doubt.

Change in a Free Economy

THE need for reexamination acquires urgency from yet another and more deep-seated source—the great changes that have been transforming our economy and that continue to transform it. For America, free enterprise has been not only a way of production, but a way of life. Today, however, this way of life differs, at least in its outward aspects, from the life of the past. How do these changes square with our basic beliefs? Do the new ways repudiate the old truths? Or have they merely brought changes of form that do not affect substance?

The principles by which America works and produces are not of today and yesterday. They have stood the test of time for generations. Yet it would be a mistake to assume that because they are fundamental, they must be changeless. It would be futile in particular to expect that the embodiment they find in our economy could somehow remain static. The only way to progress is to change. Let us look at some of the changes to which our generation has been party.

We have participated in social and economic changes that would have looked strange thirty years ago. In our day, the government has taken on by law the responsibility for keeping the economy stable and growing. Social security and un-employment insurance have become part of daily living for many of us. A heavy tax load, principally for national defense, has descended upon all.

At the same time, this age has seen a great spread in private ownership and private welfare arrangements. More than half of American families have become home owners, a great majority of adults own life insurance policies, about one-half have savings accounts, a substantial minority hold common stocks. Private health insurance, private retirement plans, even private unemployment compensation are growing all around us.

Private business itself meanwhile has not remained the same. Big business has become even bigger, but big labor has arrived and taken over some of the power and, by implication, the responsibility of leadership. Collective bargaining has firmly established itself. Business is becoming increasingly profes-sionalized and "managerial" as the separation of ownership and control advances, and has taken on new social functions in research, education, and community services. To sum up diversity under a few labels: as we have become richer, we have moved toward more government, more welfare—public and private—and more bigness.

These developments have been closely related, each one

made possible and perhaps necessary by the others. Bigness has been a necessary condition of growing wealth. High living standards demand mass production, and mass production demands big organizations. We could not hope to get the necessary capital, research, and selling by relying on small units.

The demand for welfare measures reflects both our greater wealth and the social conditions of a highly industrial and predominantly urban community. In our kind of world, many needs that in a simpler age could be taken care of more easily call for special provision. Temporarily unemployed workers cannot go home to the farm and live off the land any more—they need unemployment compensation. The aged can no longer plan to live with their children—they need social security and a retirement plan. Medical protection no longer consists of simple remedies prescribed by a kindly country doctor and available for a few cents—our higher standards call for hospitalization insurance and other forms of protection.

The growing role of government is traceable to the other changes—bigness in the private sphere, greater wealth, and the growing demand for welfare and other services. When business and labor grow and gain in power, it is almost inevitable that government should grow likewise, if it wants to keep the other two in check. Pressure generates counterpressure. The public interest, confronted with powerful private interests, has responded by building up a big and powerful government.

The social conditions created by industry and the city have likewise abetted the growth of government. The need for social services, where private action proved inadequate or too slow, has called forth public action. So have the economic fluctuations to which this industrial and urban economy has been prone. No longer are we minded to ride out major ups and downs; we have found defenses against them, at the cost of rising government activity.

Growing wealth, too, has become a motive for enlarging the sphere of government in our economy. As our income has risen, we have been able to afford more of everything. But we have not expanded our demands equally in all directions. With basic needs taken care of, it is natural that additional demand should reach out toward newer fields—luxuries, services, education, security. There is no economic law which says that a growing share of such high income needs should be supplied by government. But government abhors a vacuum and will quickly move to fill real or imagined gaps left by private enterprise. In many instances, demand seems to have been elastic in the direction of wants that government could meet, and it has met them.

These, in simplest terms, are the reasons why growing wealth seems to have been accompanied by more bigness, welfare, and government. Is this march into the future a march into socialism? In the face of the buoyant expansion of private activity and ownership, it would take more-than-average pessimism to arrive at this conclusion. The successes of capitalism since the war likewise contradict such fears. To our grandparents, perhaps, we might all appear as dangerous radicals. But a less static appraisal suggests that free enterprise has changed America, and in doing so has also shifted the old signposts.

Those who believe that our traditional values must necessarily be in conflict with such innovations overlook that the application of conservative principles does not depend so much on the "what" as the "how." Continuing social change is inevitable. That is the nature of a dynamic system. If we do not accept this, we are in conflict with the very principles we want to conserve.

Loyalty to our heritage means more than mechanically to repeat what our ancestors began. It would be futile to try to uphold traditional values by doing for the hundredth time what others did for the first. The American tradition is one of constant evolution. If we want to be like those who came before us, we must invite change as they did and break away from old patterns. Conservatism does not mean to substitute imitation for creation. It is expressed in the way in which change is brought about—step by step, relying on experience more than on theory, acting with continuity and responsibility.

This creative attitude toward the past is quite taken for granted in the operation of business enterprise. Businessmen generally are conservatives—their success, power, and responsibility all combine to make them so. Yet in order to become and remain successful, they must also be innovators. Invention, rather than market equilibrium, is the core of capitalism. One cannot revolutionize the processes of production and almost double the standard of living in each generation without setting in motion great social changes.

To try to improve upon the past does not mean to disapprove of it. There are some who, in contrast to the traditionalists, seek to justify capitalism mainly by pointing to its recent improvements. "The capitalism of the nineteenth century," they say, "was harsh, the economy of the 1920's was speculative, but now we have overcome these defects, now we have the right system." In saying so, they do injustice to the past, while also overlooking the certainty of future change. If our basic principles are sound, we may have confidence in their effectiveness today without fear of the inevitable changes, but we likewise must accept their working in the past.

Along this road that leads from the past to the future, men with different temperaments and interests will no doubt want to advance rather different distances. Men tend to be "modern" in the field in which they are specialists, more conservative outside it. This accounts for many of the differences, on social and economic matters, between academics and practical people. But whoever believes himself unalterably opposed to some kind of change has open to him a simple test. He need only ask himself whether he has ever changed his mind on a question of this nature. The world is full of people who at one time were unalterably opposed to labor unions, social security, or a flexible fiscal policy. Yet for most of them the enormities of twenty years ago have become today's matter of course. He who ever has changed his mind must beware of last ditch attitudes.

What matters is that the new propositions be guided by the old principles. We must furnish welfare without destroying initiative and provide security without doing injury to incentives. We must maintain stability without falling into regimentation and seek change without courting discontinuity. To keep initiative and incentives alive, we must be prepared to accept a certain degree of inequality in our economic fortunes, after assuring as much equality of opportunity as we can. To avoid regimentation, we must put up with some degree of uncertainty and risk. To assure continuity, our reforms should be conducted in a spirit of constructiveness and cooperation, without vindictiveness or punitive intent. If these things can be done, forms will change but substance will remain.

There is no need to labor further the idea that those wanting to conserve our basic principles must accept and even promote change. The constructive role of change is the first observation to be recorded in a reexamination of these principles. We shall pick up this thread later, but before proceeding further on our intellectual journey, it will be well to indicate some of the principal points to be touched and the conclusions likely to be reached.

॰ஓௐ

The Issues in This Book

THE substance of the economic beliefs that I would like to reexamine is not exclusively economic; it has a moral tinge. Every principle that wants to command strong allegiance must make a moral case. Men want to feel that what they are doing is useful, but they want also, and mainly, to feel that it is right.

Freedom is one of these principles. It is freedom that gives the image of a market economy, an open economy, so powerful an appeal. The belief in freedom lies at the core of our civilization. It is part of our belief in the dignity of man. Our economic system draws immense strength from this identification with our moral faiths. Because our free economy has given us an unrivaled standard of living, we have concluded, not unnaturally, that our methods are not only the "right" way for a free people, but also the most efficient way. This reaction is understandable, although one cannot help suspecting that it reflects more self-congratulation than soul searching. We should perhaps have asked ourselves whether it is really possible to have the best of everything at once. Economics rests on the proposition that to get a little more of one blessing one must accept a little less of another. Have we fallen into the trap of thinking that because we like something, it must serve us best in all possible respects?

The challenge of Communism is beginning to drive home this doubt. And our own experience confirms it. We need recall only what the nation did during two world wars. When maximum output was needed, we shifted to centralized control and direction. When the emergency was over, the shift was reversed—fortunately. The lesson is plain. A free economy can perform very well, as ours has. It can provide a rapidly rising standard of output and consumption. But if absolute maximum of output and growth is wanted there are other methods. The United States, fortunately, has never in peacetime been tempted to sell its birthright of freedom for a mess of production accelerated by forced draft methods. We have viewed economic freedom—the freedom to work and quit, to hire and fire, and to consume as we please—as part of our total freedom. We have believed—rightly, I think—that a free economy buttresses political freedom by assuring that power, freedom's eternal enemy, shall remain widely dispersed. A free economy has seemed to us a good and efficient economy, but even more it has seemed the right economy for a society of free men.

I would wish, however, that these non-material motives could have become more explicit. Freedom loving people pay themselves a poor compliment when they explain their devotion on the grounds that it is profitable. I would rather feel that I held my beliefs for their own sake and perhaps at some sacrifice in material terms. That, I believe, happens to be the truth of the matter. Freedom comes at a cost, not at a profit.

If I am right in this, our love of freedom will be put increasingly to the test as our foreign rival draws closer.

A free economy relies for its success upon the initiative displayed by millions of people and business firms, all of them representing small—sometimes perhaps not so small—centers of decision. To work effectively, these centers of decision must be powered by strong incentives. The need for initiative and incentives thus becomes the second subject of our inquiry.

We shall have to face some searching questions. The traditional view of incentives greatly oversimplifies its conclusions. That higher pay encourages more work, and that high taxes discourage enterprise is borne out only partially by available evidence. Whatever the effects of incentives, moreover, we must ask ourselves for whom they are intended and how strongly they should be applied. Should every man who earns his bread by the sweat of his brow necessarily consider himself engaged in a race with his fellow workers? Is so fiercely competitive an economy, in which a great majority must end up as losers, what we really want and actually have? Successful men may be expected to like the rules of the game by which they come out on top, and may urge all to play that game. But if the rules are too stiff, a majority of players may beg off or may decide to change them in their favor. Nor can a system where rewards are very large and penalties very severe justify itself on the grounds that true merit will always be adequately rewarded; the element of accident in economic life is too great to guarantee full justice to all competitors. Initiative and incentives are essential, but the rigors of the competitive game must be tempered to the great majority who are not likely to end up among the winners.

This view, which takes account of the different potentialities and motivations of people, will help to overcome also the image of the economy as an anonymous market in which nameless automatons pursue their bloodless advantage. The market is an essential part of a free society, but it would be a mistake to view all human action as choices among the alternatives posed by a market. Economic man responding purely to the dictates of a market may help our thinking as an abstraction. Interpreted as a reality, he becomes a menace. The center of the good society is not a bazaar.

An incentive economy—even if its rules are softened as I would suggest—is bound to produce economic inequality. To some this will appear as no more than an old fact of economic life. If they are concerned at all, they may feel that equality of opportunity, rather than of shares, is the issue. To others, inequality becomes a matter of conscience more than of economics. How can great inequality of wealth and income be squared with belief in democracy and political equality? How does it stand up before our general ideas of fairness? Inequality of wealth and income will be our final object of inquiry.

The issue has troubled men's minds since time immemorial, and while wise men may debate it, only fools will come to a final decision. To those who regard all inequality as bad, no helpful answer can be given. Others may note, however, that in a dynamic economy inequality acquires a function—it accelerates growth. By facilitating the use of incentives and the accumulation of savings, and so stimulating economic growth, inequality benefits even those who initially appear to be its victims.

In a growing economy, moreover, the parallel of political and economic inequality breaks down. One man's gain in political power is bound to be at the expense of others—his economic gain need not be. This, to my mind, removes a good part of the moral element from the issue.

Meanwhile, the growing similarity of living habits among the higher and lower income groups takes much of the edge off economic inequality. The extreme contrast of rich and poor that characterized early capitalism has vanished, and it would fulfill no function today. Equality of opportunity is also advancing, though much remains to be done.

To say a good word, howsoever qualified, on behalf of inequality nevertheless is an awkward undertaking. In the absence of other considerations, greater equality surely is to be preferred to less. Yet progressive equalization threatens harm not only to economic growth. The trend toward grey flannel conformity testifies to other dangers of equalization. Originality, excellence, and achievement in any field of endeavor are at stake. If we have needed them in the past, we can do even less without them today. The future of a free society depends on the preservation of beliefs that give room to creative inequalities.

It is into the basic beliefs of a free society in a free economy that this book proposes to inquire. Today, the survival of such a society can no longer be taken for granted. This book would argue that at a time that tries men's souls, men must go back to their first principles to see whether, in Washington's phrase, these principles still provide "a standard to which the wise and honest can repair."

II

FREEDOM AND GOVERNMENT

We have now defined a point of departure and charted a course. The decks look clear as we launch upon our first theme, Freedom and Government.

აიდ

Freedom in American Life

FREEDOM is one of the great words in our language. It stands for one of the great ideas of our civilization. It was in search of freedom that the Pilgrim Fathers left their homes for America. The authors of the Declaration of Independence put freedom directly after life itself. Today, in the great division of the world, we speak of our side as the free world.

So great has been the force of this idea that the other side has been compelled to pay it the compliment of imitation. Suitably brainwashed, the word "freedom" is now being applied to social arrangements that have no visible connection with it. To that extent, at least, the values of the West have prevailed.

Americans have always been profoundly conscious of the issues that freedom poses. If constant discussion represents

part of the eternal vigilance that is said to be the price of
freedom, we need not in this respect accuse ourselves of negli-
gence. Libraries have been written, in prose, verse and jour-
nalese. As befits a free country, ideas have differed widely.
Those who mean what they say about freedom cannot very
well insist on their own interpretation of it.

Today, the lines of debate are drawn around three important issues. The first is the very meaning of freedom. Traditionally, freedom has been thought of in terms of man's
freedom from arbitrary government. Now, it is being argued
persuasively that to the hungry man this sort of freedom is a
mockery. To be free, he needs also financial independence.
What are we to think of this "new freedom"?

Second, we have before us the familiar issue of a market
economy versus a "controlled" economy. Which will give
the better result? On one extreme are the devotees of laissez
faire; arrayed against them on the other stand the whole-
hearted planners. Most people find their place somewhere in
between. The problem is old, but new and conflicting evidence keeps coming in. We must once more define our position.

The third disputed area encompasses the role of a free economy in protecting our political freedom. Some believers in
freedom are prepared to concede that under certain conditions, a controlled economy may outperform a free market
economy. But they regard controls as too much of a threat
to liberty to take this chance. The controllers and planners, if
they see a risk at all, are willing to take it in their stride. The
issue comes to this: Is a free economy necessary—perhaps
even sufficient—as a bulwark against arbitrary power?

The issues of freedom do not date from today or yesterday.
But the acceleration of history that seems to characterize our

day, continually confronting old ideas with new situations, compels us to rethink our conclusions in each generation. Sphinxlike, history poses its riddles, and we must find workable answers if we want to live in freedom.

ᴖᴑ

The Meaning of Freedom—Old and New

"FREEDOM," said Goethe, "to be real, must constantly be reconquered." One form of reconquest, which we are practicing in our generation, is rethinking. This is entirely good and proper. If our truths are to remain creative, they must be reinterpreted to fit the changing times. An altogether unchanging truth threatens to become a dead truth.

If the "new freedom" nevertheless engenders uneasiness, it is because of the revolutionary character of the change and the ominous direction in which it seems to be leading. Does this new freedom broaden and strengthen the old, as it set out to do? Or does it decoy us where we do not want to go, toward a condition where some benevolent power guarantees everybody's freedom by organizing and regulating every minute of it?

THREE HISTORICAL VIEWS OF FREEDOM

The old freedom is a familiar thing. It centers in freedom from arbitrary power, from oppression, from violation of man's rights. Those were the realities in the days of the founding fathers. Those were the concepts of freedom that they built into the Declaration of Independence and the Constitution.

The practical statesmanship of the founding fathers was rooted in their experience of nascent Anglo-Saxon democracy. For their philosophical ideas, however, they relied heavily upon the French philosophers of the eighteenth century, such as Montesquieu, Voltaire, and Rousseau. These doctrines, formulated in the teeth of a decadent absolutism, stressed the dignity of the individual, and his freedom as part of this dignity. The rights of man were the password. Natural law was invoked in their support. Thus freedom seemed firmly founded for the ages.

This oldest defense has indeed remained a force in American feeling about freedom. It has been the force of habit rather than of reason, however. The intellectual bases of natural law have long been crumbling under a variety of attacks. The anthropologists, looking into the habits of alien cultures, have done their bit. They have shown that where we believe we see a law written in the heavens, others see nothing of the kind, or perhaps see quite a different prescription. The philosophers and social scientists have contributed their share to destroying the absolutism of natural law. Long before Einstein, philosophy and law and faith were becoming relative. A good case can still be made that freedom is a value that far transcends Western civilization. But it is hard today to regain the simple faith which natural law inspired in our ancestors.

The utilitarian philosophers and economists of eighteenth- and nineteenth-century England gave the idea of freedom a new twist. Jeremy Bentham is perhaps the foremost of this group. To them, ideas and institutions were justified insofar as they were useful. There was no need to trouble nature for an endorsement of freedom, if freedom could justify itself by its results. The invisible hand, which directed the competitive self-seeking of individuals toward the good of all, is the symbol of that line of thought.

This shift strengthened the case for freedom by putting it on a functional basis. But it reduced the stature of freedom in our moral universe, making it an instrument instead of an end in itself. And it made freedom vulnerable. If for some reason freedom should cease to be useful, humanity presumably would have no further use for it. A freedom derived from natural law, as an essential condition of the dignity of man, was exposed to no such hazard.

This opening was quickly exploited. The theory of the invisible hand, stated without qualifications, seemed a little too good to be true. An honest appraisal showed the hand to be clumsy, unsteady, and slow. Its uncontrolled manipulations caused extreme anguish to large masses of people. And the hand showed a peculiar tendency to loose its grip on freedom itself: monopoly power often came to be the reward of the successful competitor.

Withal, the invisible hand doctrine remains an important part of the intellectual foundations of economic freedom. With safeguards to preserve competition and avoid extreme business fluctuations, the competitive free market is accepted today as our basic economic principle. Jeremy Bentham's utilitarian notion that freedom is good because it is useful has survived.

A third line of argument was developed during the latter part of the nineteenth century, in the wake of Darwin's great work on evolution. "Social Darwinism" is its shorthand name, Herbert Spencer its main architect. Spencer tried to translate Darwin's ideas about natural selection and survival of the fittest into social and economic doctrine. Leave men free to fight it out, and may the best man win—that was the prescription for the improvement of mankind. Man's latest creation, the rising industrial economy, seemed a suitable substitute for God's creation as an arena for the new struggle for survival.

This unlovely doctrine, glorifying the freedom of dog to eat dog, made no major splash in the flow of Western thought. But for a while, it did exert a peculiar fascination, especially upon American thinkers. It seemed to fit the hurly-burly of post-Civil War America. For the giants that were battling their way to wealth and power, it provided a rationale that was effectively exploited.

But the analogy between the Darwinian struggle for survival and the nineteenth-century struggle to make a fortune was soon shown to be tenuous. Failure to survive in competition did not mean failure to survive biologically. It just meant survival in squalor. Poverty and disease bred more poverty and disease. Meanwhile those who survived in the competitive selection did not necessarily demonstrate fitness for anything but survival. Today, social Darwinism in the raw has few admirers. A trace of it remains, sublimated almost beyond recognition, in the doctrine that relies on competition to weed out inefficient producers.

THE NEW FREEDOM

The rethinking of freedom, which is wholesome and necessary, has borne a variety of fruit, some a little strange. On one extreme are those who, though they praise freedom, seem ready to bury it under a conglomerate of security, equality, and collectivism. Their attachment to liberty is platonic or still more remote. This type of thinking is represented by the "ultras" among American liberals, and by the left wing of the British Labor Party.

On the other extreme come the voices of a small but effective group who wants to go back to laissez faire concepts of freedom. Tyranny, they say, has once more become a mortal threat. In the shadow of this threat, they want to resurrect the ideas that were designed in days gone by to fight tyranny. The extreme right wing of American conservatives stands for these views.

In the middle, a little left of center, stand the defenders of the new freedom. Their multiform views are in no way tied to any single party line. The "new freedom" is the fruit, quite simply, of an environment that takes for granted the blessings it has and broods over those that it lacks. The new freedom is the consequence of the success of the old.

The old freedom was political: it defined the rights of man before his government. The new freedom branches out into welfare: it seeks to establish the economic rights of man. The old freedom focused upon one specific objective: to curb tyranny. The new freedom is diffuse: it finds limitations of and opportunities for freedom in many guises. Freedom with a capital "F," in fact, ceases to exist; there are only particular liberties.[1] The old freedom was mainly a "freedom from." The new freedom is mainly a "freedom to." The old freedom propounded freedom for all men: equality before the law. It was thus compatible with inequality in other respects: inequality of income, inequality of temperament, ability and desires. The new freedom regards men as free in different degrees, according to their material circumstances and their psychological make-up. Equality of freedom is possible only if we are all alike in our finances, our needs, and our desires.

By progressive relativization of the original idea, the new freedom arrives at the conclusion that freedom simply means the "absence of obstacles to the realization of desires." Unconscious as well as conscious desires enter in. Man is free to the extent that he is unfrustrated. Freedom can be achieved equally by the fulfillment or removal of desires.

This, one may surmise, is not the kind of freedom Patrick Henry had in mind when he cried "Liberty or Death." Nevertheless, the new freedom scores on a number of points when its moral and logical merits are matched against those of the old. A few examples will show why.

THE CASE FOR THE NEW FREEDOM

The old freedom protects man against oppression by the state. It does not protect him very effectively against oppression by his fellow man. True enough, it offers a formula designed to resolve such conflicts: my rights are limited by the equal rights of my neighbor. This sounds fine and works out well so long as my neighbor and I are in roughly similar positions. He owns land, so do I; we must not trespass on each other's ground, must not create nuisances, and so forth. For the rest, each of us can do with his property as he pleases.

The rule thus illustrated seems admirably clear. But what if this pretty symmetry does not prevail? Suppose my neighbor owns a factory, and I work for him. Just how is his right to do with his property as he pleases limited by mine to be treated with fairness and decency? Can he expose me to hazards of life and limb? Can he take advantage of my indigence to make my children work long hours? Can he hire and fire and meanwhile treat me exactly as suits him? If not, where is the limit to my insistence on rights that would cripple his business?

Consider a more complex arrangement than personal proprietorship, say through widely distributed stocks and bonds. How are the rights of a bondholder or stockholder limited by the equal rights of others who are not bond- or stockholders? These holdings are "property" only in a metaphorical sense— they are themselves little more than rights. It is true, then, that as a stock- or bondholder I have the right of my rights. But this formula says little about what is to be done if I en- counter some conflict of interest, for instance, with other creditors of the business, or with the public, or the govern- ment. The effort to define my rights in terms of everybody else's rights collapses in a complex society, and with it the sweet simplicity of this facet of the old freedom.

The new freedom also scores against the old in the matter of economic freedom. One need not got so far as to accept the dictum that money is crystallized freedom. But it is hard to argue that money and freedom have nothing to do with each other. The man with money in the bank can talk back to his boss better than the fellow who is just hanging on till the next paycheck. To put away some "go-to-hell money" is a good old American practice. Lack of money, like the lack of a vote, can become a source of oppression.

There is an answer, of course: in a free society, everybody can make money enough to protect this part of his freedom. The freedom to earn one's freedom always exists. In this basic sense, inequalities of income create no permanent dis- parities of freedom, so long as there is equality of opportunity. But this is a partial answer only, showing that each man can eventually solve his own problem. As of each moment, we must admit that differences of wealth do influence our free- dom. If we deny this, we make ourselves vulnerable to Anatole France's retort about the majestic impartiality of the law that makes begging and sleeping under bridges illegal for rich and poor alike.

Economic insecurity, moreover, poses still another threat

to freedom. It may inspire demands for state action that in turn may jeopardize freedom. Men will die for freedom but they will not necessarily starve for it. A society that wants to be free must not expose its members to this alternative.

THE CASE AGAINST THE NEW FREEDOM

This much it is necessary to concede to the new freedom: freedom is not simple, it is complex and multiform. And it is not purely political, but has a pecuniary side. Many proponents of the new freedom probably mean no more than this. With them there is no dispute. But if we take it at its word, the new freedom goes much further.

Definitions, like comparisons, are odious. Whoever is looking for an argument need only try to define a familiar term. But more than odious, definitions are also insidious. They carry inside them, like the apple its seed, the conclusions at which one eventually is to arrive. This is egregiously true of the new freedom and of the definition cited above: absence of obstacles to the realization of desires. Though its spokesmen may not be aware of it and would probably disagree if it were pointed out to them, this version of freedom points fatally toward collectivism.

Freedom so conceived means, in effect, that man is ninety per cent unfree. The vast majority of our desires are inherently condemned to remain unsatisfied. This is so only in part because, in the words of the radio sage, most good things in life are either immoral, unhealthy, or fattening. Even our legitimate desires, whatever fraction of the total they may be, must very largely remain frustrated. Economists have agreed since time immemorial that man's wants are virtually limitless, and hence usually well beyond his pocketbook. And even more conclusively: one cannot do everything at once. Although we had the money, we would not have the time to do all we want, be it in a day or in a lifetime.

Given an unrealizable picture of freedom, the collectivist conclusion follows naturally. Man is largely unfree; if the government does something to reduce his freedom still further, it really is not making a very basic change in his condition. Let the government proceed then.

The same conclusion is reached by another route. To regard freedom as the ability to realize desires makes freedom virtually the same thing as purchasing power and power in general. Let us overlook the peculiar twist by which freedom, normally thought of as the antithesis of power, is turned into its synonym. Let us also overlook the deflation of a once noble idea that follows from its association with purchasing power. We cannot, however, close our eyes to the results. The desire for freedom in the old sense is the strongest objection to a centrally controlled economy. Even if that economy could be made to function properly, it might cost us a good part of our freedom, and we do not want to take that chance. But if freedom means purchasing power, a well-oiled centralized economy might increase it. Why object to it? Such are the rewards of making freedom serve as a ringer for the econo- mists' old-fashioned word "utility."

This, however, is not the end. The government can come in by still another door. The new freedom is relative. It can be increased either by more satisfaction or by less desire. To in- crease satisfactions is a slow process. How about working from the other end? "Man is rich in proportion to the things he can leave alone," said Thoreau. Why not let the govern- ment drill its people in the pursuit of this kind of wealth? The cause of freedom might advance more rapidly that way.

Nikita Khrushchev's claim that the Russian citizen enjoys more freedom than the American might make sense in those terms.

I have absolutely no intention of identifying the spokesmen of the new freedom with the foregoing argument. But such, it seems to me, are the policy implications of their thought. When we approach the end of the road we are within hailing distance of George Orwell's "Freedom is Slavery," the maxim of Airstrip Number One in *1984*.

The relativist twist of the new freedom, which allows freedom to be advanced by fewer desires as well as more fulfillment, has further curious overtones. Not only does it invite the government to enrich our freedom by training us to the thin life. It is hard to reconcile with the meaning of evolution and with the dignity of man. Life has evolved from the simple to the differentiated, from the undemanding amoeba to pretentious and exacting man. In the course of this evolution, the proportion of frustrated desires undoubtedly has grown enormously. Has evolution moved in the wrong direction? Ought we to reverse ourselves and hasten back toward a more amoeba-like condition? Or ought we to found the dignity of man on the belief that the more differentiated is superior to the simpler model?

The new freedom, in short, is one of those dangerous grounds where some nuggets of truth are to be garnered at great risk. Some of its contentions must be accepted. But its ultimate meaning is of a sort that many of its own spokemen would resist.

HOW SERIOUSLY DO WE TAKE OUR FREEDOM?

There are some difficult problems ahead also for the supporters of our present kind of freedom, which lies somewhere between the old and the new. They can be reduced to one simple soul-searcher: how seriously do we take our freedom? When we talk about the American Way of Life, we automatically list freedom high among its blessings. Are we sure that this is more than a gesture?

Let us call the roll of the lovers of freedom. Here is the American business man. He rises to the heights of eloquence when his freedom from public regulation and intervention is at stake. He is less inspired when the talk is of antitrust action. The tariff, according to him, does not appear to enter into freedom at all—exception made of some notable captains of industry who have spoken boldly against the tariff.

Here is American labor. Labor favors free enterprise, and why shouldn't it, since most private employers are easier to cope with than Uncle Sam. But labor does not hesitate to upset the free apple cart by coersive union practices or inflationary wage demands. Nor does it seem to see a threat to freedom in urging that controls be put on business.

Here is the American intellectual. He is the number one beneficiary of a free system, by whose freedom of expression he makes his living. In a dictatorship, the great bulk of intellectuals would be silenced or made to say and write things they did not believe. No group has more to lose from a loss of freedom than the intellectual. Yet even he is giving ground. On the right wing, he has yielded to the temptation to exploit political sentiment in order to discredit progressives. On the opposite side he has not been above resorting to social pressure as a means of silencing non-conformists. We have come a long way from Voltaire's "I disapprove of what you say, but I will defend to the death your right to say it."

Last but certainly not least, here is the great American public. Since its first year in grade school, the American public knows that liberty is the priceless heritage which we all must defend. And whenever the public becomes aware of some restraint of freedom that it regards as a nuisance—be it no worse than fluoridation or parking regulations—it is prompt to rise to freedom's defense. But on occasions such as presidential elections, little more than half of the voting population think it worthwhile to exercise their freedom, as shown by the record of the last seven elections. Residence requirements and restriction of the Negro vote in some states account for only a small part of this electoral absenteeism. And when some unfortunate gangster, movie writer, or professor gets caught in the limelight of investigation and the issue of civil rights is posed, the public is rarely on the side of the angels who are said to protect even the fallen. The public's love of freedom, like that of smaller groups, is sadly selective.

This lack of positive enthusiasm for the principle of freedom is not all. In the air there is something the flavor of which is caught in Erich Fromm's phrase "Escape from Freedom" or in Sartre's "Man is condemned to be free." We sense it in a seeping away of individualism. Eulogists of teamwork and cooperation are making the lone wolf look like a regular outcast. The "other-directed" man is taking the place of the "inner-directed," as conformity is replacing conscience. Suitably camouflaged by grey flannel, this trend gathers momentum without ever coming to the head-on collision with our ideals of freedom that one should think inevitable. Growing numbers are jumping on the bandwagon. Is modern life getting too much for us?

If not too much, life certainly is getting to be more of everything. Science continually widens the range of possibilities and in that sense increases our freedom. More and more options are open to us, as technology stretches the horizon of action and as the pecuniary potential of the individual increases. Add to this the sense of insecurity that, according to the sociologists, springs from the contemporary flux of habits and beliefs, and it is not surprising that we react with a voluntary curtailment of freedom. The uneasiness that the widening range of choices engenders drives us toward some protective cover.

The individualist will regret this conformist trend. It obviously does not follow the line of freedom. But it may well represent a piece of practical wisdom. Freedom is known as a heady draught, and not infrequently its admirers have overestimated their capacity. If today we seem to be rationing ourselves to a more modest rate of intake, we are strengthening our defenses against the dangers of instability and friction that lurk in a very free world, a world that may be becoming all engine and no brakes. As the world fills up with people, as life becomes more complex and closely knit, freewheeling individualism becomes increasingly hard to live with. Some restraints are clearly needed. The danger is that in our search for stability and belonging we may give up more freedom than we intended to.

I repeat: how seriously do we take our freedom? Our preceding brief glance at American business, labor, intellectuals, and general public conveyed no impressive picture. Freedom in the abstract clearly has a hard time competing with peoples' pocketbook interests, their prejudices, and even their apathy. Where any of these are at stake, freedom often comes off second best. But the battles of freedom fortunately are not all fought on grounds of general principle.

They also take the form of debate over some specific restraint or irritation. And here, as we know, Americans in all walks of life are quick to respond. Americans are intolerant of nuisances. They will fight vocally and valiantly for their removal, and in doing so they often fight for freedom. Painfully slow progress in giving reality to our principles by enactment of civil rights legislation has left most of us mortifyingly undisturbed. But when the public after the war had become tired of price controls, rationing, and black markets, the government was compelled to remove them.

The daily conduct of the American people does not lend much support to the doctrine that freedom must be protected as a natural right. Our conduct does seem imbued with the implicit belief that freedom is good because it suits us. So long as the American people insist on the luxury of not having to tolerate nuisances, so long will they preserve for themselves a fair measure of freedom.

ᵔᵔᵔ

Economic Freedom versus Organization

WE HAVE now acquitted ourselves of our first responsibility to freedom—an inquiry into its meaning. We proceed to look into some of its uses. Our faith in freedom rests in part, as we have noted, upon the belief that freedom is economically useful. This belief needs to be put to the test.

Over a hundred years ago, Karl Marx announced to an unsuspecting world that capitalism was doomed. Capitalism, said the Manifesto, would drag the masses deeper and deeper into misery and would eventually break down under the pressure of its inconsistencies. Ever since, undisturbed by the evidence, Marx's disciples have kept repeating that capitalism cannot work.

In 1917, the system that Marx thought superior was inaugurated in Russia. This set capitalist sages to proving more energetically than ever that Communism cannot work. Communism meanwhile has conquered almost half the population of the world. Russia, starting practically from scratch, has become the world's second industrial power. Yet until the Soviets put Sputnik in orbit, the chorus that the communist system is ineffectual droned on. We fell into the error of copying our critics, in believing that something cannot be true because we do not like it.

In entering upon our discussion of the relative merits of a free and a controlled economy, I shall try to stay away from words like "cannot" and "must." Nor shall I appeal to history for any binding generalization. History proves that things can happen, not that they must. I shall try to weigh strength and weakness, and in doing so endeavor to give the Devil his due, however little I wish to have to do with him. Economic effectiveness is one thing and the good life is another.

THE STRENGTH OF A FREE ECONOMY

What makes a free economy? First of all, a free economy is a decentralized economy. Decentralization means that we have millions of centers of initiative, instead of only one. It means variety that stimulates creative thinking. "Crazy ideas" have a chance that might never survive scrutiny by an entrenched bureaucracy. Decentralization means making the fullest use of our individual capacities.

Next, a free economy relies upon free markets to decide what is to be produced, instead of upon a central authority. The market gives the economy high flexibility, and makes it responsive to consumer wishes. If consumer wishes are to rule

—and what else should in a free economy?—the free market offers the best means for the allocation of productive resources.

In the third place, a free economy relies heavily on incentives and competition. It offers to reward each according to his contribution, and it holds out exceptional prizes to the exceptional man. Competition stimulates each to do his utmost.⌐

Decentralization, free markets, incentives and competition are the basic mechanisms of a free economy. The more freedom allowed, one must assume, the more intensive and effective will be the work of these mechanisms. It is noteworthy, therefore, that in practice we rather pointedly refrain from pushing freedom as far as it will go. If we felt that no other system had comparable advantages, that presumably is what we ought to do. We would want an economy consisting mainly of very small units, in order to have as many centers of initiative and sources of ideas as possible. This kind of economy would also give us perfectly competitive free markets and would hold out the unique incentive of everybody being able to become his own boss. Is it only perverseness, or the scheming of selfish interests, that blocks such wholesome extension of freedom?

Of course it is not, and most of us are perfectly satisfied to see economic freedom restrained in some respects. ⌐The uses of freedom have their limits. Competing with the principle of decentralization is its opposite, organization, as represented by big business. Big business has always been credited with the special advantages arising from mass production. Today, however, big business also claims pre-eminence in two other respects: research, and the ability to finance large investment expenditures to realize upon its research. Much is made of these advantages of big business in contemporary literature.[2] It is refreshing to hear such forthright speech on behalf of a sector of the economy that until recently preferred to keep itself under wraps. But we must be alive to its meaning. The claims of big business severely cramp the style of several familiar figures: the independent inventor in his attic or garage, the young man striking out for himself in a free competitive market, the small business man who is often said to be the backbone of the American economy. They are all manifestations of the freedom we extol in a sense in which big business is not. To the extent that we accept the superiority of the big corporation, we agree that there are economic forces more powerful than sheer freedom.

Especially intriguing is big business' claim to superiority in the financing of capital formation. The claim can hardly be denied. Big business has better access to the capital market, and it often can finance its expenditures from undistributed profits. But in driving home its superiority in capital formation, big business touches the Achilles heel of the free and completely decentralized economy. The speed with which capital is accumulated in such an economy is unpredictable. Rapid accumulation is possible, but it is not part of the logic of the system. The decentralized system can promise a strong flow of inventions, and efficiency in the use of resources. These are, as it were, among its built-in features. Up to a point, inventions also probably set in motion forces that generate additional savings. But in the main, the flow of savings is regulated by the tastes of the people in the community. The system merely interprets these tastes through the market. It is not the fault of the sysem if people decide to consume all of their income, nor can it claim credit if they save a high proportion. It works just as efficiently in one case as in the other.

A high rate of saving and a high rate of technological advance are the joint promoters of economic progress, with technology probably the senior partner of the firm. Since the decentralized system can promise the second, but not the first, it can guarantee some progress, but not necessarily at the fastest rate. In practice we have enjoyed very satisfactory progress, because invention has been accompanied by a high rate of business saving, and because we have been willing to save as consumers. But the consumer is not entirely reliable as a source of savings. Big business, by reminding us of its superior power of capital formation, points up one of the advantages that a more highly organized system enjoys over a more decentralized.

As it stands today, our economic system is a combination of the elements of decentralization and organization. We have not pushed freedom to its ultimate limits, but have taken it, as a good thing should be taken, in moderation. This poses some ticklish questions. We are pretty sure that our system contains the right ingredients, but how about the proportions? If we had to do it over, would we order "the mixture as before?" And supposing, as I do, that we would, why do we like this particular combination of freedom and organization? Is it because we feel that it is the most productive combination? Or do we prefer it because we like freedom for its own sake, and insist on a certain substantial amount of it even though production could be increased by adding more organization to the formula? In other words, is there one optimum formula if we care mostly about production, and another if we care mostly about freedom? If so, which of the two formulas are we using, the productive or the free? If we are closer to the free formula, how much production are we giving up as the price of freedom?

These questions go to the heart of the role of economic freedom in American life. To give an honest answer, we must turn to the fully organized and controlled economy and see what alternatives and possibilities would confront us there. Of course the issue is not whether socialism is advisable for the United States. As of today and I hope many tomorrows, it is out of the question. A small modification of the formula, a slightly different combination of freedom and organization, is all that need be contemplated. But the principle of organization is best observed where it flowers in its purest form.

OUR ARGUMENT WITH SOCIALISM

For many years, almost everybody in America was sure of one fact about socialism—it didn't work. If ever there was a case where it was not safe to be sure, this was it. Russia had demonstrated to us repeatedly that to say that something cannot work or cannot be done is not a promising gambit in a progressive world. At the beginning of the war, it was widely said that Russia could not hold out for long. After the war, we were sure she could not develop nuclear weapons for many years. It took the launching of Sputnik to convince many former sceptics of the economic and technological potential of the Russian system.

In addition to closing our eyes for too long to Russian accomplishments, we have been guilty also of closing our minds to the menacing power of Marxist doctrine. Those who have said that the philosophy of Communism consists in keeping the people in poverty, so that poverty may keep them in Communism, show little perception of the intellectual capacity of their adversary. Communism is a formidable intellectual structure, built by first-rate minds over many decades, with an inner logic and consistency that capitalism might envy. The average American, debating with a Russian the merits of their respective systems, would soon find himself in hot water, unless he were exceptionally nimble. An American economist facing a trained Marxist dialectitian might find the going even harder.

Yet in our post-Sputnik awakening, the pendulum may well have swung too far. Some of us today seem overimpressed with the achievement of the Russians to the point of believing that everything is possible to them, that they can do nothing wrong —in short, that every Russian is seven feet tall. The obvious fact that we want to keep in perspective is that their system has its considerable elements of strength, and also its considerable elements of weakness. We shall have occasion to note both as we pass muster of the principal objections that have been raised in the West to the extreme forms of economic organization that go by the name of socialism or communism.

The economist's argument with socialism proceeds on a somewhat abstract but quite straightforward plane. Some have argued that it is bound to be grossly inefficient in the use of resources. Others concede that it may have certain short-run advantages, but believe that it would tend to stagnate in the long run. A widely held view says that a socialist economy is bound to be authoritarian, militarist, and hostile to the needs of the consumer. Let us take these points one by one.

Is Socialism Necessarily Inefficient?

The view that a socialist economy is bound to be grossly inefficient usually refers to the absence of free markets and free prices. In the absence of free price movements serving as indicators of demand and supply, how are the planners to know what is wanted and how it should be produced? In the absence of a market mechanism that adjusts wages and interest to the productivity of labor and capital, how are the planners to know how much of each to use? In a market economy, there will be a price on capital and on labor, in accordance with their respective productivity and with the demand for and supply of each throughout the economy. Total demand will absorb total supply.

In a socialist economy, wages and interest presumably are fixed arbitrarily, if interest is calculated at all. Suppose the planners now proceed, as business men would, to plan production by using the cheapest combination of labor and capital. If labor is relatively cheap, they plan to use more labor, and vice versa. But with prices of labor and capital fixed arbitrarily, the planners will probably find that they planned to use more labor than is available while available capital remains unused, or the reverse. To find the wage rates and the interest rates that will allow both factors of production to be used to the full is impossible without a free market. So runs the argument.

The difficulty is real, but it need not be overwhelming. Even in our economy the market works far from perfectly, yet we seem to manage fairly well. And in a socialist economy, as has been shown by numerous students of this obstruse problem, the price setting function of the market can be approximated in one way or another. Modern computing equipment no doubt would facilitate such calculations. There is a question, of course, whether a socialist economy will in fact proceed in this way and revise its prices frequently or whether it will increasingly let itself drift into a rigid pattern of unrealistic pricing. The possibility of rational use of resources, at any rate, can hardly be denied.

On top of this basic difficulty, it is observed, a socialist economy must face a host of more practical problems. A huge bureaucracy, extreme centralization, loss of individual initiative, loss of incentives, are among the most obvious. How real these difficulties are is demonstrated by the Russians' efforts to decentralize their operations. The aggressive use of incentives, in conflict with the communist objective of income according to needs, testifies to the same effect. Very probably these difficulties are a major drag upon any socialist economy. But quite possibly they can be mitigated, or compensated by advantages in other directions. One is hardly justified in asserting, on the basis of such cogitations, that a socialist economy "cannot work."

Must A Centralized Economy Stagnate?

The second objection, on grounds of long-run stagnation, makes a subtler case, besides having the virtue, for the prognosticator, of not being susceptible of immediate verification. Bureaucracies, it is argued, tend to be static and self-perpetuating, unwilling to tolerate outsiders, and constitutionally disinclined to experiment. Omnipotent bureaucracy runs the risk of choking off original thought. When bureaucracy does innovate, it is sorely tempted to ease the repercussions upon sectors that stand to be hurt, in the familiar fashion of the welfare state. The economy will gradually tie itself up in a web of restrictive, protective arrangements. Progress will come to a halt.

This is an interesting and plausible speculation. It is challenged, but not necessarily disproved, by the speed of the Russian advance in science and technology, and by their complete ruthlessness in dealing with groups that stood in the way of what they considered progress. The Russian bureaucracy has not yet had time to mellow and ossify. And it has enjoyed the tremendous advantage of being able to borrow ideas and techniques from abroad.

Yet one cannot help wondering when one learns about the massive resources that the Russians are investing in research, and the serried ranks of newly trained engineers that they send into their factories. This is not the stuff of which stagnation is made. And though party line discipline may curb new ideas, it need not interfere with the routine of progress, the "habit of innovation" that can be acquired. All one can say of the stagnation thesis is: There may be truth in it, there may even quite likely be truth in it, but there need not be enough truth to turn the scales.

Must The Centralized Economy Be Militarist And Hostile To The Consumer?

A third group of objections culminates in the assertion that a socialist economy must become authoritarian, militarist, and hostile to consumer interests. I shall postpone momentarily the first of these points, the alleged inevitability of dictatorship. It is by far the most important contention and requires a careful look. Let us suppose for a moment that we are in fact speaking of a dictatorship. That kind of system has historically often been predisposed toward the other two—militarism and hostility to consumer interests. The various elements in the picture all re-enforce one another. It usually suits a dictatorship to whip the people into line by dressing up alleged enemies abroad. The appearance of these foreign enemies then makes it necessary to concentrate on armaments and heavy industry. Concentration on armaments and heavy industry is convenient, in turn, because that kind of production lends itself more readily to planning than does a more differentiated output for consumption, while planning errors that occur can be concealed more successfully. Finally, sitting on the consumer also serves the useful purpose of keeping him from getting soft and from demanding leisure that he might misuse to think deviationist thoughts.

Small dictatorships may find the military posture unconvincing nowadays. But there are other means of withholding the economy's surplus from the consumer. Monumental buildings, roads, multiplication of long-run projects, and conspicuous investment of all sorts commend themselves. So long as the state and its leaders are exalted at the expense of the citizen, an arrangement competent dictators usually find convenient, the consumer will be shortchanged. Something like an iron law of exploitation seems to weigh upon societies that have lost their freedom: if they are not exploited for one purpose, they will be for another, but exploited they always will be.

This chain of argument is plausible, and richly illustrated by contemporary experience. But not all of its links hold equally well. Consumers have, after all, enjoyed a considerable measure of progress in the Iron Curtain countries. In Hitler's Germany, mass living standards in 1938-1939 probably exceeded the best years of the Weimar Republic and of Imperial Germany, despite the priority of guns over butter.

The repression of the consumer assumed to be typical of this kind of economy signifies something else. The less there is of his, the more there is of the state's. If the state employs these resources productively, it can speed up the rate of progress beyond what could be done through investment from voluntary savings. Part of the forced savings may of course end up in late model military hardware that will soon join earlier models on the scrap heap. But even the most entrenched militarists know that they need an economic base. Investment in steel, oil, and other basic industries will therefore be pushed even by a militarist regime. If militarism is only a sideline, the capital goods industries can be expanded further to produce more equipment to expand the capital goods industries still further to produce still more equipment—and so on.

The wartime experience of the United States is a case in point. We are ourselves on record, as regards the effectiveness of a dictatorial system, with actions that speak louder than many words—the nation's actions in two world wars. When the pressure was on, there never existed any doubt what had to be done; the United States shifted from a free system to controls. Patriotism made Americans willing to tolerate the severe repression of consumption that went with this system. There was no opportunity to discover what would have happened if the wartime system had been perpetuated, fortunately. But while it lasted, it delivered the goods.

Forced draft methods like these may build up an industrial structure in ten years that would take twenty-five years by voluntary means. If at the end of some reasonable period production is switched to consumer goods, the consumer may even feel that the horse cure was worthwhile. Most of the totalitarian economies promise that this switch will be made at an opportune moment. None, so far as I know, has as yet found the moment opportune. One can understand that it would rather go against their grain, and suspects that they would run into great political as well as economic difficulties if they tried. But meanwhile the capacities of some of these economies are growing at an impressive and alarming rate.

Democratic Socialism—The Worst of Two Worlds?

The rapid growth potential of the centrally controlled economy hinges on one condition: the use of force. A centralized system that is undemocratic, dictatorial, and relies on force against its own people has two great advantages: It can extort more savings, and it need not worry about how to arrive at and execute a general plan that is acceptable to a majority. A centralized economy run on democratic lines will have to shift into a very different key.

Democratic socialism can accumulate capital to the extent that the citizens allow resources to be diverted from current consumption. The citizens may wish the government to invest much or little, but in any case they will very probably yield up less than could be invested were the government prepared to override and repress their consumption urges. This is the first problem of democratic socialism and of any form of democratic centralization.

Contemporary experience shows that a democratic country with a highly centralized economy can invest a good deal— witness the much cited case of Norway. But Norway is a small country operating under perhaps exceptional conditions. The experience of other countries that have gone in for some degree of planning during shorter or longer periods suggests that consumers may make demands upon their government that leave inadequate amounts for investment. The adequacy of capital formation in a democratically planned country rates a large question mark.

It is true that big corporations owned by the government— railroads and utilities, for instance—might use their power for the purpose of forming capital just as big privately owned corporations do now. In practice, however, nationalized industries seem to have been used more often to subsidize the consumer than to extract forced savings from him. The United States Post Office Department, with its perpetual tendency toward deficits, illustrates this point in our own context. Compared with the dictatorial economy's capacity for massive capital formation, democratic socialism appears weak in this sector. Quite likely it would prove inferior also to a free economy.

The second problem of reconciling democracy and effective central planning—always assuming that the dilemma is not

resolved by escape into authoritarianism—will be encountered
when the time comes to agree on a plan. A group of competent
technicians would no doubt be able to draw up a consistent
plan that should work out tolerably well, provided they can
be guided by economic considerations alone. But what if they
are exposed to all the pressures of a political democracy?
In a free economy, the painful decisions are made anony-
mously—by the market. In a democratically planned economy, somebody must take responsibility for them—unless he
can take the line of least resistance and avoid them. The
chances are that decisions will be designed, not to achieve the
maximum benefit to the whole, but the minimum injury to
any one, perhaps with special benefits thrown in for special
interest groups. In this dilemma, all pressures combine to avoid
readjustments, shore up losing situations with subsidies, and
generally do things the easier rather than the better way. To
overstrain resources would be a permanent temptation. If the
political process were of the nature of the American, with
unlimited opportunities for amendment of the administration's
proposals by the legislature, the "plan" as finally voted might
not even be internally consistent.

The special frictions of planning and centralization might
to some extent be offset by gains from more intensive organization. But the analogy between the step from small business to
big business and from big business to big government misleads.
The first step lifts the economy to a new level of productivity.
But beyond a size that varies for particular industries, increases
in the scale of mass production fail to pay off noticeably. We
have no clear indication that the step to big government would
create productivity gains that would make up for the handicaps of democratic planning.

Democratic planning probably would score high in maintaining economic stability. Though changes in tastes and techniques are bound to bring some fluctuations, these ought not to develop into cumulative depressions. Employment, whether productive or not, should usually be full if the planners make that their principal goal. Not so long ago we might have rated the capacity to avoid depressions a major advantage of a planned over a free economy. After the experience of the last fifteen years, we may perhaps allow ourselves to think that the difference on this score need not be very great.

THE OUTCOME OF THE DEBATE

I have tried to present a view of the relative merits of three economic systems: the free economy as we have it (with considerable admixture of government) in the United States, the dictatorial centralized economy typified by Russia, and the democratic centralized economy, which was approached, although perhaps remotely, by some European countries in the years following the war. In comparison with the free economy, the Russian system shows elements of decided strength. Its power to extort savings from the consumer and to carry out plans without opposition gives it an advantage that may overcome grave handicaps in other respects. If we reject this system, as we most decidedly do, we must found our rejection on our attachment to freedom, not on economic grounds. To argue otherwise can only confuse our own thinking. Good causes are hurt by bad arguments. And as between reasons based on belief in freedom, and reasons based on economics, the appeal to freedom strikes me as the more attractive. We want freedom, and we are willing to pay an economic price for it, by sacrificing the larger output that we might have in a forced draft economy.

As we look at our own free economy, we must draw a

similar distinction between our motives rooted in freedom and those rooted in economics. If we wanted to push freedom to its farthest limits, we would move toward some kind of Jeffersonian society of small independent farmers, shopkeepers, and artisans. Because a pastoral society of this sort would make a very ineffective economy, we are glad to stay with big business. We are willing to sacrifice some freedom for the sake of economic gain, even though we draw the line long before we reach anything resembling a centralized economy.

By claiming, as we so often do, that our free economy maximizes everything at once—the enjoyment of freedom itself, present living standards, and future progress, we render freedom a poor service. We are implying that we are really making no sacrifice for freedom. We are getting it cheap, almost as a by-product. The truth is otherwise. Freedom has its cost and it is our good fortune that we are able and willing to pay it.

Then what of the democratic centralized economy? How does it compare with our free system? Properly implemented, it would have its strong points—large-scale organization and good prospects of avoiding major economic fluctuations. On these scores, however, a free economy today can offer close competition. The principal drawbacks might be the need to please everybody, which would turn every economic decision into a political compromise, the tendency to overstrain its resources, and especially the difficulty of forming capital in the teeth of a clamorous consumer demand. The democratically controlled centralized economy lacks the power of ruthless capital formation of the first and the incentives and the unbiased judgment of the market that propel the other. Thus it might find itself outdistanced by both the dictatorial and the free model.

This judgment of the democratically controlled economy

seems to be borne out by postwar experience, which has given pause even to previously enthusiastic planners. The course of true planning never seems to have run smooth. The difficulties encountered by the European countries that went in—quite moderately—for planned economies, the successes of the free economies, and the good record of our own economy seem to have raised the stock of free markets. The once-bright promises have begun to pall and the belief that "planning will make it so" is waning. Today, a quarter-century after the big depression, the case for a free economy once more is strong.

This preference for a free over a democratically planned economy can be established, I believe, on economic grounds alone. But there are others. Although so far we have never witnessed a verification of the prediction that democratic planning, goaded by its frustrations, will turn to dictatorship as its ultima ratio, the planners have not altogether succeeded in cleansing themselves of this unpleasant suspicion. This is a possibility that so far we have deliberately excluded from our weighing of pros and cons. Now we shall probe a little more deeply into the relations between economic freedom, political freedom, and planning.

ᘓᖡᖱ

A Free Economy for Political Freedom

As TIMES change, cause and effect change with them. During the eighteenth and nineteenth centuries, the then liberals demanded political freedom because they believed it would lead to a free economy. Today, the argument has been reversed. A free economy, it is said, constitutes a bulwark of our political liberties. I shall not try to investigate whether those who advocate a free economy as a means to a political end are uniformly more interested in the end than in the means. We shall take the contention at face value and analyze its merits.

How does a free economy defend political freedom? The contention points two ways. One line of attack drives home the danger that a centralized economy may (dogmatists say "must") slide off into totalitarianism. This is the negative side of the argument. The other line argues the positive virtues of free enterprise in dispersing power, checking the government, and strengthening the sinews of democracy. The first of these themes—the alleged affinity of centralization and totalitarianism—has been sounded briefly in an earlier phase of our discussion. We must now deal with it at greater length.

PLANNING IN FREEDOM?

"In social evolution," says Friedrich Hayek in his *Road to Serfdom*, "nothing is inevitable but thinking makes it so."[3] This applies eminently, I believe, to Hayek's own social argument of the alleged totalitarian effects of centralization. They are not inevitable. True enough, planning is probably much harder without dictatorship. In consequence, it is likely to be much worse and less effective. But there is no compelling reason why a nation strongly imbued with a democratic tradition should not succeed in maintaining its freedom under planning. Among the three possible roads that democratic planning might take—the road to serfdom, the return to free markets, or simply the unchanging route of continued democratic planning—none seem to be prima facie ruled out.

The experience of Great Britain illustrates all three eventualities. Under the Labor Government, some degree of democratic planning held sway, with no striking success and with some abridgement of economic freedom through rationing, production controls, and exorbitant taxation. Political freedom was not impaired, though something that might eventually have become an authoritarian trend could perhaps be discerned when in 1947 the government obtained the power to control the free movement of labor. Here the prophets of democratic doom came closest to proving their case. But the government reversed itself, perhaps under the prodding of some inner voice, or perhaps of that of the rank and file. Ever since, and contrary to the prophets, Britain has backed away from centralized planning toward freer markets.

Let us follow the supposed march into socialism step by step. How far could the dismantling of economic freedom go, before the man in the street would feel seriously incommoded? First to go would be the business man's freedom, and with it probably his ability to make and keep large amounts of money. The business man can be relied upon to be vocal in his own defense. But whether his protestations would find much of an echo among the lower income groups is debatable. Next in line, if the planning screws are tightened, is the consumer. He would find his range of choice narrowed, through import restrictions, rationing, standardization, and perhaps heavier taxation. Here popular resistance might be expected. If postwar experience in the United States is any guide, strong consumer restraints are not well received by the American public. In some European countries, on the other hand, people seem to have taken queing up without much protestation so long as the rations were adequate.

The next turn of the screw, if there is one, would probably squeeze labor. After production and consumption controls loom controls over manpower. Manpower controls are at the watershed between economic and political freedom. Here is where the British planners suffered their Waterloo. If manpower controls can be made to stick, any further tightening seems to lead into clear civil rights territory. Wide administrative discretion, severe penalties for noncompliance, efforts to whip up support and stifle opposition, may become necessary to back up the controls. What still separates us at this point from Soviet or Nazi style practices is the power of the people to change the government if this kind of planning does not suit them. How real a power is it?

Leftwingers argue that it is adequate, and that it is all that matters. Because they tend to identify freedom with security and welfare, they are undismayed by loss of choice and opportunity. Because not a few of them are technicians, they are impatient of imperfections and compromises. For many, this means impatience with the free market, with indirect fiscal and monetary controls, and with the political process. "Ye shall know controls, and controls shall make ye free."

Their embattled libertarian opponents dispute this case. They deny that an ultimate right to recall the government means much in the way of democracy or freedom. They argue that the mere formulation of detailed plans implies far-reaching delegation of power to the bureaucracy. Without this delegation, planning is likely to amount to no more than governmental rubber-stamping of whatever the market decides. The execution of the plans, if it is to be possible at all, will require that even more discretion be entrusted to the bureaucrats, and very able bureaucrats at that. To plan is human, to fulfill divine—or nearly so.

The powers of the legislature, therefore—so the libertarian argument goes on—are progressively watered down. Popular government becomes a figurehead, like some princes of old, manipulated by powerful major-domos. A change of government, under such conditions, will not bring a real turn of the tide, campaign oratory to the contrary not withstanding. The great powers of the administration, indeed, may make it increasingly difficult to mount an effective opposition. People know where their bread is buttered, however stingily, and dare not risk real opposition. The great weight of the decisions to be made, that reach deep into everybody's life, make issues tense and compromises problematical. Strong authority, the libertarians continue, beckons as a way out. Dictatorship, of course, does not solve problems, but it can liquidate them. Democracy, when it cannot solve them, must find a way to survive them. Life with major unresolved problems may become so uncomfortable that democracy breaks down.

Tension under planning, the libertarians say, may destroy democracy in yet another way. If the issues at stake threaten the very way of life of some group, that group may refuse to accept the verdict of the democratic process and resort to force. Rumblings along these lines have occasionally been heard from the left wing of European socialist parties. When we arrive at this margin of intolerance, dictatorship may prove the last refuge of a planner.

The old-fashioned liberal's case against the centralized economy is a persuasive one. It is marred, however, by the frequent use of the word "must" where "may" would be more appropriate. History, which can prove no rules but often does prove the exceptions, has already handed down rebuttals to the indictment, as in the cases of Britain, the Scandinavian countries, and Australia. In these and other countries much exposed to planning, democracy and freedom have survived without serious difficulty.

Hayek, in appraising the evident fact that the British did not travel down the road to serfdom, stresses what he calls the softening of the British character under the Labor Government. Thus he shifts his apprehensions to the long run.[4] I would argue that a case that may be almost watertight in countries where democracy and freedom are weak does not necessarily apply to countries where both are strong. A vigorous people that knows its mind and how to speak it is not likely to let its planners run away with the economy. It will want them to submit to existing habits, tastes, and prejudices. It will expect them to be nice to the consumer. It will expect them to be particularly nice, in an expensive way, to special interest groups. It will expect the planners, in fact, to do the very things that snarl up an economy in special privileges, restrictions, and over-organization, and that hold up progress.

This gentle kind of planning seems entirely compatible with freedom. The people of the country so governed might find that though their life was not bad, it was curiously slow in getting better. They might come to believe that dilatory progress was the price of liberty, a penalty they would willingly go on paying to protect their freedom. Or they might decide to shift to a freer economy.

THE POLITICAL CONSEQUENCES OF A FREE ECONOMY

We have tried, in the preceding pages, to do justice to the view that a centralized economy must necessarily end up as a dictatorship. It is a view that does not stand up under dispassionate analysis. There is danger, but not certainty. The indictment against centralization is not that it confronts us with one inevitable evil. More likely it confronts us with the choice between two. The centralized economy need not be

THE COST OF FREEDOM

totalitarian, it may just not be very effective. That is the negative side of the argument about the interaction of economic and political freedom. Let us now turn to the positive side, which asserts that if we have economic freedom, political freedom is thereby strengthened. How much weight does this assertion carry?

WHAT USE DO WE MAKE OF OUR ECONOMIC FREEDOM?

Free economic choice is an important part of our total store of freedom. This consumer freedom, to be sure, is a rather prosaic version of our great ideal. The unobserving may be pardoned if he fails to recognize the housewife pushing her truck in the supermarket as a present-day incarnation of the goddess of liberty. Yet this is the shape of things to come or already arrived. Where tyrants rule, liberty is high drama. Where the drama has reached its happy end, liberty becomes habitual and a little dull. It nonetheless remains liberty.

This freedom of the supermarket and the department store is increasing rapidly in our day. That is true at least of the lower income groups, for which technology opens up ever-widening consumer options. The reverse probably applies to the upper incomes, whose choice of custom-made clothes and furniture, of individualized styles of living, is being narrowed down by high wages and standardization. At all levels, however, mass production and big business are taking a certain toll of consumer freedom. In the United States we have the biggest automobile industry in the world and the smallest choice of domestically made cars. Compare this with the richly varied automotive fauna that lends enchantment to European roads. We are sacrificing, or are made to sacrifice, some possible freedom in favor of greater plenty.

Today it is sometimes argued that aggressive advertising

interferes with the consumer's free choice. Without this artificial stimulus, it is said, he might make different choices, and possibly he would have fewer wants. I am not sure whether this proposition is true as to facts—the degree of influence of advertising—but in any case I think it is of limited relevance in a discussion of consumer freedom. Advertisers, who might be pardoned for exaggerating the effectiveness of their devices, say that it is very difficult to make a customer buy something he positively does not want. If all that advertising does is to awaken latent desires—what influences that play upon us since childhood do not? Is education an interference with freedom? Or does it, rather, by indoctrinating the child, open for him the door to a vastly wider range of choices? Advertising undoubtedly biases consumer choice. I find it hard to believe that it materially reduces consumer freedom.

Free consumer choice is not a monopoly of a free economy, of course. It cannot honestly be argued that a centralized economy must inevitably reduce consumer freedom. Wherever there is democracy, consumers are likely to insist on a fair deal. But what can be said is that consumer freedom does not come naturally to a planned economy. The natural drift of a planned economy is the other way, and the force of economic gravity must consciously be checked by democracy. The centralized economy puts a strain upon democracy and freedom; the free economy does not.

Freedom Needs Exercise

No statistics have so far been developed to show which of his various freedoms the average American exercises oftenest. But it is a fair guess that economic choice, if it does not rank first, runs a close second to free speech, as exercised in the form of griping and "shooting off our mouths." This habit of a constructive use of freedom is important. The price of freedom is not only eternal vigilance, but also eternal exercise. Free elections are fine too, but against a centralized government that thinks it has a mandate or, still worse, a mission until the next vote count, they may be a little thin. I have already ventured some doubts about the picture of a nation that obediently queues up for four years, coupons in hand, and at the end of the planning period rises up and votes the rascals out of office. It is just possible that the habit of acting as one is planned to act may carry over into the political sphere. People accustomed to getting what they want for their money are more likely to insist on the same for their vote.

This case is not invalidated by the fact that many economic choices are reserved to only a small part of the population—to the business man making his decisions as producer. Freedom of the press, too, is used by only a few, and to the full only by a small sector of the press—usually a few scandal sheets. In either case, the government is broken in to the salutary habit of respecting its citizens. Freedom needs exercise.

THE DISPERSION OF POWER

Power is the great enemy of freedom. Throughout American history, liberals and conservatives alike have feared and sought to guard against concentration of power. In the political field, dispersion of power has been attained through the threefold division of the federal government, and through the balance among federal, state, and local powers. Economic power has been held in check through competition and the free market. Absence of economic power reduces political power. Thus competition becomes the classical mechanism through which a free economy upholds political liberty.

Today, we are not so sure that this mechanism is in working order. The picture of our big corporations and their leaders as powerless pawns moved about by the invisible hand of competition is not convincing. Our big labor leaders and farm leaders do not even pretend that they have no power. Power is bursting out at every seam of our economy. Can we still trust a free economy to fulfill its political mission?

In the midst of present-day enthusiasm over bigness, these are unpleasant questions. They have not gone, however, without attempts at an answer. On one side are those who, like former Council of Economic Advisers Chairman Edwin Nourse, are profoundly fearful of the big pressure groups. They see the Leviathans in battle and fear that both victory and stalemate will crush free institutions. Others have seen, in this power-block warfare, a continuation of competition with other means. John Kenneth Galbraith's doctrine of "countervailing power" is the standard around which the optimists have gathered. Market power, it is argued, tends to create its own checks and balances. Where there is market power, someone is getting away with something. Where that happens someone else is ready to muscle in on the surplus.

Thus, the market power of a big food processor is checked by that of a big chain store. The market power of a steel producer is checked by that of an automobile company. The market power of big business in general is checked by that of big labor. So it goes. Wherever power begins to concentrate, it calls into being new power to balance it. The citizen and his government, far from having to worry about being trampled to death by the giants, must speed up the growth of countervailing power. Galbraith views the New Deal and its labor and farm legislation as a large-scale exercise in building countervailing power.

In this manner, the balance of power substitutes for the equilibrium of competition. How perfect a substitute it is remains debatable. I may be pardoned if I prefer the peaceful company of a hill of ants to that of two bulls who for the time being cannot hurt me because they have locked horns. Who is to assure me that the dominant characteristics of Galbraith's economy will be those of balance rather than of a battle field? Galbraith himself draws attention to various limitations of his doctrine. Yet it has the merit, at least, of offering a self-perpetuating mechanism. Whenever the balance of power is destroyed by the victory of one side, Galbraith argues, a new power will form to challenge the winner. There is hope, therefore, that balance may be maintained under the system of countervailing power no less than under competition.

The theory of countervailing power is a bold conception. It helps to fill the gap left, in the ideology of freedom, by our declining faith in the universal rule of competition. For unless we can rely upon some automatic mechanism to check and disperse it, we must somehow come to terms with power. It is only realistic to admit that some measure of private power is always bound to exist. But without the dispersing mechanism, all that stands between the citizen and the power blocks is the sense of responsibility of the holders of power. Faced with this prospect, the citizen might prefer to trust himself to the tender mercies of big government. To say that this meant committing suicide for fear of death would no doubt overstate the case. But it would nevertheless signify a risk, if not an actual surrender of freedom. As long as there is hope that power may prove self-neutralizing, there is no need to take this jump.

One event of recent years has brought home sharply the

value of even an imperfect dispersal of power: the activities of the late Senator McCarthy. As a result of his investigations, a number of able people lost their jobs in the government. Many of them found a haven somewhere in the anonymous reaches of the free market. In this curious way, persons who may not have been extreme admirers of free enterprise were led to discover one of its advantages. So long as power remains dispersed, the power to fire is not the power to destroy.

This shifting mechanism, this ability to get out from under, means something even in less dramatic situations. To know that one is locked in is uncomfortable even to those who do not want to leave. Awareness on the part of the holders of power that the exits are open is a strong check to its abuse. The consumer who can take his custom elsewhere, the worker who can check out and go, are symbols of freedom protected by the dispersal of power.

Freedom As Insurance

Does all of this add up to proof positive that a free economy is necessary for political freedom? Surely it does not. We cannot stand up and assert unconditionally that our political freedom will suffer if we compromise our economic freedom. Neither can we claim that a free economy is ironclad protection against political tyranny. The man who is sure that one or the other must be so is sure only to be wrong in this particular. All we can do is to weigh the chances, and arrive at our own judgment.

Freedom is like health—it is taken for granted while one has it. One becomes aware of it when it is gone. The temptation with either is to disregard it, to drive health and freedom too hard in pursuit of objectives that may turn out to be at their expense. Doctors urge us to take care of our health at some cost of time, money, and more interesting activities. Our analysis of freedom tells us that we must promote freedom at the expense of certain alternative goals if we do not want to run a risk which, however hard to measure, clearly exists.

We have already tried to appraise this risk element. Small abridgements of freedom can come easily—many people will not mind them if they do. The risk of total loss of freedom is small, but the penalty is terrific if it happens. The loss may well be irredeemable; dictators play for keeps, and there may be no second chance. As we look away in space and time from our country where everything seems so safe, we are reminded that most of the people have been governed badly most of the time. Democracy and freedom have so far been minute exceptions in a world where the rule is the rule of force.

To the risk conscious, the case for taking out substantial insurance on freedom must seem strong. The nature of the coin in which we may have to pay will not always be the same. It may be efficiency, it may be immediate progress, it may be stability or equality. Gains in all of these could perhaps be had—of this, too, we can never be sure—at the cost of a little freedom here and there, or at the risk of a major loss of freedom. And of course we are already giving up some hypothetical freedom for some of the other blessings we want. The question is how to balance the accounts.

The answer would not be easy even if we could count on an exact quid pro quo—such and such freedoms for so and so much stability, equality, growth and efficiency. But of course that is for the most part not so. The problem in the main is one of risk and insurance. We must weigh the cost of giving up some benefits, themselves not certain, as insurance premiums against the small risk of major disaster to freedom. The danger that we shall under-insure is considerable. Unlike the risks of fire and accident, the vision of danger is not always clearly in our minds. It needs an effort to visualize it. Unlike casualty insurance, the premium is not collected once every year. It will take frequent check-ups to keep our insurance up to the mark.

∽∞

Policies for Freedom

CHINESE wisdom has it that it is better to speak the truth than try to remember what one said. Sometimes, however, even what one believes to be the truth can be hard to remember. Our discussion has been complex and full of qualifications. Let us recapitulate the main points.

THE ARGUMENT THUS FAR

Freedom, we agreed, will normally give us a high rate of economic progress, because it quickens thought and initiative. The uses of freedom, however, are not unlimited. We would not want an economy made up wholly of small businesses. Though this would offer the highest degree of freedom it would cost us the advantages of bigness. No free economy, moreover, can guarantee as high a rate of capital formation as a dictatorial economy that is prepared to squeeze forced savings out of the consumer. If this economy succeeds in suppressing freedom sufficiently to push through its plans, it may progress more rapidly and steadily. Our rejection of this kind of system must rest therefore not upon its alleged ineffectiveness. We dislike it quite simply for what it is. If this means paying a price for freedom, we are willing to pay it.

This same conclusion was reached by still another route. Not every centrally controlled economy, we saw, must necessarily be dictatorial. Planning in freedom is conceivable. But the economic effectiveness of this system must seem dubious so long as it remains democratic and free, and if it tries to become more effective, it may well have to become less free. A free economy sidesteps this risk. At the same time it invigorates our political freedom, by dispersing power and by strengthening our habit of meeting our own problems. We may have to endure a slightly higher measure of insecurity and instability. If so, these sacrifices are a kind of risk premium to insure freedom against the accidents to which it is liable under another system.

POLICY LINES

Experience is our euphemism for the mistakes we have made, policy for those we are about to make. Yet people who never make mistakes are not as smart as they think. We must make up our minds and run our risks.

Our problem is how and where to draw the lines that limit power. Where, in the interests of freedom, should government leave off and private action begin? Where, within our American government, should the dividing line run between federal and local authority? Where, among private organizations, do the blessings of bigness cease to compensate for its risks? Of these three dividing lines, the most important is of course that which defines the proper sphere of government.

One thing is so obvious that perhaps it is in some danger of being overlooked. The lines to be drawn, imprecise as they are, will not stay put through the years. Everybody will agree to this in principle. Yet much of the excitement over "government intervention" and "interference" originates from the inevitable shifting of the lines. Let us for a moment consider this evolution—we need not dignify it with the word "historical law."

There are many who believe that the sphere of government is expanding perpetually. Fifty, a hundred, or two-hundred years hence we shall inevitably end up in full blown socialism. This is the view not only of all Marxists and many liberals, but—unadvertised—of a good number of conservatives.

Yet even if this were accepted beyond doubt, our questions about where to draw the line today would remain. To know the end of the road does not compel us to go there right away. One could accept socialism as the ultimate outcome in the fullness of time and yet believe that for the time being we have gone farther than we should. Those who regard society as an organism will object to speeding up its evolution beyond its natural rate.

But the prognosis of inevitable socialism is itself subject to question. The trend of the last fifty or one-hundred years undoubtedly has gone in the direction of ever-increasing government power. Trends by themselves, however, prove no more than "so far so good." History has often been unkind to prophets who relied on extrapolation, and may reverse herself as she has so often done. The rise of capitalism is itself the result of such a reversal, which broke up the omnipotent autocracies of the seventeenth and eighteenth centuries. The pendulum does not always swing just one way.

Another view, associated with the name of Karl Mannheim, seeks to explain just these swings of the pendulum. It argues, quite simply, that government will always extend its power as far as its physical means of control will reach. Thomas Jefferson expressed this apprehension when he said "the natural progress of things is for liberty to yield and government to gain ground." During the nineteenth century, the flexibility and growing complexity of private enterprise outdistanced the administrative ability of government. Now government is catching up with a vengeance. Better transportation, communication, computing equipment, have shifted the balance to its advantage. They have made possible new techniques of controlling production and distribution. With the increase in the government's opportunities for power, the exercise of that power follows automatically.

If this gloomy theory should be valid, one would have to anticipate that what happens to the business man on one day would befall the man in the street the next day. Mass propaganda, brain washing, and advanced police methods are recent developments that could be employed to bring home to the citizen the glories of the up-to-date state. One vainly tries to imagine the technological developments that once more might give the individual the edge over his government.

This, however, is one more deterministic view of history that, like other historical "laws," may eventually be repealed by history. History, the view of a great industrialist notwithstanding, is certainly not bunk, but "laws of history" sometimes are. Apocalyptic visions can lead to interesting theories, but they are poor guides to practical action. To define the role of government in today's economy, we need not speculate whether a hundred years from now the government will have absorbed the whole economy or not. What we must do is to note the changes that are occuring in the economy today, and to trace our lines of demarcation along the grain of those facts.

In drawing up a bill of contemporary particulars for this purpose, it is difficult to deny that the demand for more government action is often irresistible.

Item one: A world full of tensions that compel us to maintain costly defenses. The economist is tempted to define this away as a special situation, and to want to discuss the role of government "ex-defense." But our defense needs are very much a part of our life, and they push the government deeply into the economy.

Item two: The changing structure of our economy. We are over a century removed from the nation of small traders, farmers, and artisans which was the United States in its early years. Ours is a predominantly urban, industrialized economy, with all the problems which are the incidental products of that blessed state—in their technical, social, and economic forms. These things have no laissez faire solutions.

Item three: We are getting very rich. With rising income, as I have noted above, the demand for some goods and services (e.g., luxuries) rises faster than for others (e.g., basic foods). As it happens, some of the services of which the government is the chief provider—though by no means all—exhibit this elastic demand: social insurance, education, public works.

These and similar inescapable facts explain why the line that circumscribes the role of government has not been held in our time, and why it may well be pushed further. In a good many respects, the government probably has been crowding the private sector unnecessarily. In others, where private action is less practicable, more may have to be done. Those who look at some present trends from the viewpoint of the past complain of "socialism." I think they are mistaken. What we are witnessing today is in its larger part not a movement to the left nor the right. It is an adaption of a growing economy to new conditions of its own making. This adaption we must welcome. To forestall it might produce tensions beyond the point of economic and social tolerance. I do not venture to predict what the future movement of the line between the public and the private sector may be—where it may bulge, where retreat, whether it ever will come to a standstill or someday perhaps even begin to shrink all round. I argue that much of the movement of recent years has been inevitable and good. I would argue further that the line between private and public, local and federal should be drawn, always, with the realization that not only economics but freedom is involved.

NO MAGIC FORMULA

We shall briefly pass muster of a few general formulae that have commended themselves to some for drawing the line between the public and the private sector.

One familiar formula is laissez faire. It is so much at odds with contemporary reality that to support it would be tantamount to joining a suicide club, even if its claim to provide a natural dividing line could be upheld. But in fact laissez faire provides no such line. Its few proponents argue that to enjoy a "natural" state of freedom we need only establish full freedom of contract. The government's role would be happily limited to the enforcement of these contracts. In this "night watchman state," everybody would then be free to buy, sell, hire, fire, work, and quit as he pleased and contracted. Our problem of defining the economic functions of government would be solved by eliminating them.

We need not concern ourselves here with the general objection to laissez faire, which has to do with the sort of "contracts" that people who have bargaining power would offer to those who have none, and with the possibly very erratic functioning of that kind of economy. At this point, our objection must be of another sort. It is that this "natural" dividing line between the public and the private sphere is not natural at all. It is the result of laws and institutions just as "artificial," i.e., man-made, as any other rules by which we might work. The laws that protect property, the laws that discourage the use of physical force as a method of bargaining, may have seemed rather unnatural to some when they first began to be recognized. One can visualize the robber barons of old in their eyries complaining bitterly about government interference with their old and natural right to waylay traveling merchants. Any demarcation line is bound to be artificial—it follows the laws of man, not of nature. What we call laissez faire are just the regulations to which we are accustomed.

A second proposal for drawing the line between the public and the private sector relies on the use of some mechanical rule of thumb. Let us make it a rule, say its proponents, to hold government expenditures to some understandable benchmark. This benchmark might be so and so many dollars per head of the population, such per cent of the national income, or some similar standard. The exact figures would be drawn from current practice. At a time when public expenditures threatened to get out of control, this device might have its merits—if it could be upheld. In the longer run little could be said for it as a manifestation of good economics. There is nothing sacred about any fixed amount or proportion. One that makes sense today may not do so tomorrow. A formula is no substitute for judgment.

A third expedient is to make an itemized list of the legitimate economic activities of the government and to check off existing practices against it. Two forms of "intervention" are generally accepted today as legitimate—in fact as essential for the health of our system. One is stabilization of the business cycle (alias full employment policy). The other is maintenance of competition and free markets. To these, most of us would add the provision of some measure of social security, the "floor over the pit of personal disaster." We would probably add the conservation and development of natural resources; this has been a traditional preoccupation of the American government. We might add the development of these resources and of special industrial potentialities, as in the atomic energy field, if they exceed the capacity of private business. We might further add the socialization of certain forms of property risk. We have undertaken this for home owners through the FHA (Federal Housing Administration), and for bank depositors through the FDIC (Federal Deposit Insurance Corporation).

This "itemized list" approach is concrete and realistic. Its difficulty comes from its failure to exclude anything inherently. Everybody can load the list with his pet projects. In the end it may read like a list of programs in the federal budget. To take inventory of what we are doing and call it policy is a familiar practice, but not good policy.

Finally, there remains the venerable formula of Abraham Lincoln that the government should do for the people only what the people could not do or could not do so well for themselves. This phrase partakes of a timeless wisdom that can always be endowed with the contemporary meaning that conditions require. Applied meaningfully, it lays down a standard of action and a means of drawing a line, according to the circumstances of the day, beyond which government should not trespass.

One qualification I would venture to add, however, to Lincoln's formula. It would have to be shown that the people could do something only very imperfectly, and the government very substantially better, before the government should step in. This caveat follows from our earlier discussion of the price that we should be willing to pay for a little extra freedom, for an extra margin of safety. In our day, more perhaps than in Lincoln's, the government can do many things a little better than the people. It can always provide cheaper financing, thanks to the superior rating of the public credit. Hence public power, for instance, can usually be sold cheaper than private power. Government, moreover, often can command where private enterprise must bargain. Hence a far-flung enterprise like that run by the Atomic Energy Commission may be more effectively run by public authority than by private business. Big government, finally, can promise to perform functions with a high degree of honesty that may become badly snarled when allowed to get into local politics. Project for project, dollar for dollar, the federal government may quite often have an edge over the people.

But this project-for-project, dollar-for-dollar analysis is incomplete. It overlooks a heavy mortgage in terms of indirect costs and disadvantages. This is not the place to discuss the cumulative discouragement of private and local initiative that follows successive expansionary steps of the central power, however important they may be. The cumulative softening up of freedom is what must concern us, the easy surrenders on minor issues, the weakening of the defenses against a big assault that probably will never come, but that cannot be ruled out altogether.

Freedom is everybody's business, and hence often ends up by becoming nobody's business. Whoever becomes alarmed about it runs the risk of becoming an alarmist. We have always enjoyed such large reserves of democratic strength and freedom that a serious threat could hardly be conceived. We can say "it can't happen here" with scarcely a touch of irony in our voice. Yet who is to tell us that there cannot be a "man on a white horse" in another long war, in another big depression? On previous occasions our democratic defenses were in such good shape that they took totalitarian pressures with barely a quiver. Will they always be if there should be repetitions?

Although it goes against the economist's grain to say it, the conclusion seems clear: We must do some things less efficiently than we might. We can well afford to—the extra cost is not likely to be high in a country where private and local initiative are strong. This means such things as giving private power a break, knowing it may cost more. It means surrendering some federal oil and mineral reserves to private exploitation, even though the government might possibly retain them to some greater future advantage. It means letting the private mortgage market do the bulk of real estate financing, even though the government could perhaps do it more cheaply. It means private medical service and insurance, although a public health service might in some ways be more economical.

Within the government sphere, the same principle applies. "Local if possible, federal if necessary" should be the watchword. Whatever can be done locally, with reasonable competence, should be, despite the very understandable groans of impatient perfectionists. For private business this means a broader range of opportunities, but also of obligations. In particular, business would be ill-advised to act the dog in the manger and claim that unless something is done privately, it should not be done at all. In keeping the private sphere as large as possible we aim to protect freedom, not business. The purpose is to build character, not profits.

In practice, all that can be done to strengthen freedom is likely to be marginal. We cannot and do not want to remake the country economically and politically to guard against intangible threats to freedom, any more than we are going to remake it geographically to reduce vulnerability to nuclear attack. But a steady awareness in marginal decisions of the demands of freedom is necessary. "When in doubt, stick to principle." This means everybody. If laissez faire is no good, laissez George le faire is no good either. What we do not decide ourselves will inevitably be decided for us by others. Freedom means not to have this happen.

III

INITIATIVE AND INCENTIVES

The theme of the preceding pages was the meaning of a free economy. The modern conservative believes that it is an effective economy. But he is not compelled to rationalize himself into believing that it is the most effective of all possible economies. His faith in a free economy rises from another source. Human freedom, political freedom, assurance against a system that "pushes people around," appears to him intimately bound up with economic freedom. Free enterprise, to him, is a way of life more than of making a living. It is on the "free" more than on the "economy" that he rests his case.

A World of "Challenge and Response"

A FREE economy means a decentralized economy. A system so constituted will work poorly unless the actors display a high order of initiative and drive. Its sponsors are committed, therefore, to a strategy of powerful incentives. To be successful, a free economy must be an incentive economy. The accent thus placed upon man and his plural, people, is something of an act of faith. In performing it, free enterprise runs the same risks as democracy. If people do not perform, democracy and free enterprise will not perform either.

But the risk is not entirely uncalculated. Only the sorest of misanthropes will quarrel with the statement that man is our most important economic resource. Man is not only the end of economic life, he is also the beginning. When he bestirs himself, he can do much under unpromising conditions; when he doesn't, favorable conditions are of little use. Few differences are greater than that between a man who is trying hard and one who is not. The success of a capitalist society depends on making it worth a man's while to try.

Modern conservatives, however, like an incentive economy not only because they hope it will make the wheels hum. They believe, perhaps somewhat optimistically, in its human virtues. They do not yield to liberals in their concern for man. But where the liberal seems to express his feelings by making things as easy for man as possible, the conservative believes in giving him a taste of the strenuous life, to put muscle on his character.

Lest this suggest overtones of "survival of the fittest," "social Darwinism," and other jungle jargon, let me enter an immediate disclaimer. In the age of welfare capitalism, few modern conservatives believe in these things, and hardly any say them. But there is undoubtedly a difference between them and liberals in the degree of firmness and softness with which they want to see people treated.

To make his case on this point, the conservative is compelled to appeal to history, past and future. Those who fix their eyes on the present are usually inclined to discount the stern lesson and the grim moral. For the time being, they are often right. But in the longer perspective, the proportions change. The conservative takes the long view, beyond short-run ups and downs toward the far vistas of time. Over these great distances, he sees dangers as well as great promise. He would like to have the team that is to make the trip keep in first-rate condition.

His long perspective inclines the conservative toward the secular analysis of historians like Toynbee, economists like Schumpeter. For Toynbee, the simple mechanism of incentive, initiative and effort is the fundamental law of life.[1] He looks upon the history of nations and civilizations as a succession of challenges—dangers, opportunities, problems—that may or may not be met by response. As long as a community remains healthy, it will surmount most challenges. Eventually, however, it deteriorates, through internal conflicts, soft living, or apathy. Then one day it fails to meet a challenge and begins to go downhill to its final extinction.

Schumpeter, who wrote before Toynbee, analyzed economic progress in terms that embody much the same principle.[2] He saw the economy carried forward mainly by the entrepreneur, the business man with vision. The entrepreneur took advantage of new opportunities—inventions, markets, techniques—which others had not been able to grasp. His action is a response to the challenge of opportunity. For him as for Toynbee, the key to progress and survival is initiative responding to incentives.

Both Toynbee and Schumpeter have been criticized by experts who point out that reality does not work quite in this way. The experts no doubt are right. Great general theories always distort reality. But in a broad sense, it seems clear that Toynbee and Schumpeter pointed to an important principle. Unfortunately these great truths about human initiative, incentive and performance degenerate quickly into

the kind of Fourth of July oratory to which so many of us
have become allergic. Fourth of July speeches are fine; certainly they are inevitable. And they obviously must refer to
the great truths and symbols of our civilization. But they
render these truths and symbols a poor service, at least in the
minds of thoughtful people. A truth turned into a slogan by
repetition does not become any less true, it only becomes less
convincing. Repeated ad nauseam it begins to provoke positive
resistance.

Initiative, incentive and performance have been among the
chief victims of this process. Their plight is worsened by the
fact that at a strictly scientific level, not much can be said
about them. Even where performance can be measured—in
terms of hours, or of output—social scientists as yet know
little about what causes it. But the most important aspects
cannot even be measured—they are qualitative. Everybody
knows that there are more ways than one to spend eight
hours at a job. Everybody knows that a man can work far
below, as well as above, his rated capacity. But there is no
yardstick for such performance, and for the circumstances
that call it forth. Lack of measurement contributes to a widespread scepticism about initiative and incentives, and a willingness to accept policies hostile to them.

What makes a man respond or not respond to a challenge?
For part of the answer, we must look to man himself. "The
fault, dear Brutus, is not in our stars, but in ourselves . . ."
Human capacity to respond to challenge no doubt varies
greatly from one person to the next. There is little evidence,
however, that it varies greatly among nations or races. If
Americans have shown unusual initiative, it has largely been
due to their earthly environment and their institutions, if not
to their stars. Environment and institutions can be created.

What are the conditions likely to elicit initiative and effort, among a group of men not exclusively modeled on Kipling's "If"? As I see them, they are freedom, competition, and incentives in the narrower sense. Freedom is the first ingredient of an invigorating climate. Freedom, both when it exists and when it is being fought for, has brought creative thought and action into bloom. We have dealt with its double role as an end and as a means in an earlier chapter. There is no need to pursue this familiar avenue further—here for once all Western opinion arrives at a common ground.

The second great driving force in our environment is competition. Competition does not mean quite the same thing to business men and to economists. I am using the term in the sense of the business man, who sees General Motors and Ford as fierce competitors, not of the economist, who would not be altogether sure. Competition of this sort has been a great force for achievement in America. It is incentive, in the sense both of reward and of penalty, of carrot and of stick. It is a major theme which we shall have to leave to the next chapter. Here I just want to stress its importance for an incentive economy.

This leaves us with incentives in the narrower sense as the third element in the triad of forces upon which we rely to call forth initiative and effort. On these—the kind of reward offered, the prospects of winning, the kind of people to whom they appeal, the nature of the responses—we shall concentrate for the rest of this chapter.

ᴄᴏ₼ᴏ

Non-economic Incentives

WHAT kind of incentives? To argue the importance of human effort, as I have done so far, involves the risk of carrying coals to Newcastle. A socialist would hardly disagree, though he might draw different conclusions from the premise. To a conservative, the conclusions seem to point toward the need for strong incentives.

First, however, let us guard against erroneous impressions and exorcise immediately the specter of economic man. No economist has ever met him, and few would enjoy the experience if they did. But his shadow sometimes seems to fall over discussions of this kind. Obviously, neither our activities nor our incentives are exclusively or even predominantly economic. Man, like Cleopatra, is a creature of infinite variety. He needs activities, outlets, affections, satisfactions that lie far removed from the economic sphere. He is beset by pressures and problems that income and wealth cannot solve.

Old Jeremy Bentham, the spiritual father of economic man, would probably have agreed heartily with these propositions. He might have gone on to argue that human needs and problems, however diverse, could always be dealt with by rational action. He might have underrated the emotional, the irrational, in his fellow being's make up. Today we probably know more about the human psyche, its need for adjustment and for a sense of belonging. These satisfactions cannot come by way of reward from a system of economic incentives and penalties. If the incentive system ignores this, it may do more harm than good. It must not monopolize the stage and must not crowd other values into the background.

The rejection of economic man means something further. Even the incentives cannot be wholly economic. All forms of power and prestige, of sense of accomplishment, teamwork and service enter in, probably more importantly in the upper reaches of hierarchy. And there are all the lesser trappings for the younger set—the office rug, the desk placed catty corner, the private water pitcher, and whatever invidious distinctions an up-to-date personnel department can devise.

All this is commonplace. But the moral that seems to follow is perhaps less wellworn: if non-economic incentives are powerful, how essential are the purely financial? And is there a case for arguing that, with increasing material progress, incentives should become increasingly non-material? Some present personnel practices seem to point in that direction. We seem to be regretting—and perhaps reversing—the democratic decision of the founding fathers which deprived us of nobility, titles, honors, and decorations as an inexpensive means of extracting high performance.

There is no use pretending, however, that financial rewards do not count. The futility of that pretense is sure to be endorsed by every young man who finds himself promoted to a new job with more status but no more pay, even though the personnel department would like him to think otherwise. In contemporary America, the young man is right, and the personnel department had better recognize it. The materialistic element is strong in our civilization, as it had to be if we were to make economic progress. To perform well economically, a society must appreciate worldly goods. Once it has acquired the taste, it will be receptive to and demand economic incentives.

The materialist side of America has been held up to much scorn and ridicule. We may agree that it is nothing to be particularly proud of. But it has a function. If America should never make any other contribution to civilization than to abolish poverty at home and show the way to abolishing it abroad, history will not close her books on our country with a deficit.

✑

Some Evidence on Incentives

IF WE are to pass judgment on the effectiveness of incentives, we must first see how they function. We shall first look at incentives to work, next at incentives to save.

WORK INCENTIVES

It may come as a shock to many that the broadest and simplest of incentives—higher pay—very likely has a negative effect. If we raise everybody's pay and expect everybody to work harder, we shall probably be disappointed. The evidence is not conclusive, but it leads one to suspect that a general increase in pay produces, sooner or later, a cut in the amount of work done. Over the years, certainly, rising wages have steadily been accompanied by shorter hours. The wage contracts bargained out periodically by unions and management carry the same message: higher pay goes hand in hand with shorter hours.

The negative response is perfectly understandable. A higher

rate of pay makes work more attractive, which seems to imply that longer hours will be worked. But a higher rate of pay also means a higher income, and this in turn may dispose the recipient to sacrifice a little income for a little more leisure. The balance of forces may turn either way, but the evidence suggests that it will usually be toward more leisure. An extreme instance is the primitive individual who works to feed his family and to provide himself with liquor or other simple amusement, and who quits on the day of the week when he has achieved his two-fold objective. Evidence of this sort of response abounds.

How far the more sophisticated worker is removed from a similar reaction seems to depend upon the temptations in his life. If the economy puts enough of them within his reach—home, car, household goods—he may not feel what economists have seen fit to call the "diminishing utility of income" as quickly as when these incentive goods are lacking. But he too will, in the long run, probably demand shorter hours as his wages go up. To make him work more, extra pay for overtime is needed. Here the balance of attraction turns in favor of additional effort, because the increase for overtime is substantial, while his total income goes up only moderately.

Across-the-board pay increases, then, seem to be incentives in reverse. Fortunately this disappointing conclusion does not apply when we look at the hierarchy of jobs. A group of men may work no more or no harder when the pay of all goes up. But if only one man out of the group can be promoted to a bigger and better paying job, there will be competition. The nature of the group will determine how many will compete. At the lower levels, perhaps only a small fraction will feel the challenge. In a management group, the response may be universal. In either case, effort is extracted from several men, although the reward goes to only one. Evidently differentiation is the secret of effective incentives—the creation of distinctions that give rise to emulation and invidious comparison, to use Veblen's favorite idea. The positive side of these is initiative, effort, and performance.

We have some concrete knowledge about these responses from studies of the effect of taxation upon the willingness to work and invest. Here we have incentives working in reverse, as it were. Has the rise of tax rates, at the same time as it raised blood pressures, lowered work incentives? Has it perhaps forced some men to work and invest more aggressively in order to maintain accustomed living standards? The surveys seem to show, as usual, a wide variety of reactions. Many of those interviewed thought that for themselves or their firms high taxes did not affect the willingness of executives to work at their existing jobs. A few believed that there was a positive effect—executives worked harder in order to maintain their standard of living as taxes kept rising. A few had the opposite experience.

It was on the fringes that taxation mainly seemed to tell. Here and there someone had refused to take a better paid job with another company because taxes made the difference negligible. Occasionally, men had refused to take on heavier responsibilities for the same reason. Some older executives had retired prematurely. Firms recruiting trainees for management jobs sometimes had encountered a rather muted response to their offers.

Crawford Greenewalt, President of Du Pont, speaking before a Congressional committee, cut through many of the ifs and buts of the argument by simply asserting that business men now in the mill would not drive themselves any less hard because of high taxes. High taxes hurt, but the compulsions of the job were stronger. The problems that high taxes created were in the future: The difficulty of getting a large enough group of good candidates from whom the next generation of executives would be selected.

Mr. Greenewalt's apprehensions are confirmed by what William Whyte, Jr., has to say in *The Organization Man* about the new generation of management trainees. Whyte depicts with some awe the grueling pace of the contemporary executive, listens to his lament over high taxes, and concludes that they do not affect his performance. But the new generation is different. Whether because of taxes or for other reasons, they are not disposed to kill themselves at their job. Perhaps they may yet end up doing as their predecessors did. But perhaps not.

One impression emerges: The effect of financial incentives upon executive effort lends itself splendidly to the full-throated assertions of conflicting conclusions. Those who question the need for strong incentives and who deny the adverse efforts of high taxes can point to a large majority of business men as exhibits for their thesis. Mr. Greenewalt does not need $500,-000 a year to run Du Pont. He has said as much himself. Incentive payments, therefore, largely go to waste. That is one possible conclusion.

Those who believe in incentives need not be discouraged by the evidence. In many markets, the majority of sellers are getting more than what they would be willing to close for. But the market can offer only one price for one product, and that price is needed to attract the marginal supply. If the marginal supply is essential, the price must be paid. The market for executive talent is of a special sort, but broadly speaking, it supplies us with the number and quality of executives that we have because of the price they can command in money, prestige, collateral advantages. If we had been in the habit of paying them more, we probably would have more good executives. If we pay them less, or take away more through taxes, we probably shall have fewer.

There may be a chance of getting more without paying more—through education. Only about one half of all highly qualified high school graduates find their way to college. Yet it is in the colleges where the talent scouts of business do their hunting. If all qualified young men went to college and were exposed to the talent scouts' gaze, Mr. Greenewalt's problem of finding enough trainees at moderate post-tax pay might be solved.

There is much to be said for this approach. That every man should get the education he is capable of ought to go without saying in a country that believes in equality of opportunity. To make this point, it is not necessary to appeal to the need for more executive material. But that more education would fully solve the executive supply problem is far from certain.

Lack of a college education will keep a man from becoming a professor. It will keep him from becoming a lawyer, or a doctor. It will not keep a first-rate man from becoming a top executive. Our economy, whatever else its imperfections, has not yet become so immobile and stratified as to prevent promotion from the ranks. What education *can* hope to do is to provide more executives who are adequate. It is unlikely to provide a great many more who are topnotch.

Aside from this, the power of colleges to turn out topnotch executives seems to be waning, if William Whyte's observations hold. According to Whyte, the new young men do not plan to buck for the top jobs. They mainly want good jobs, and of these they feel pretty sure. How far this attitude reflects the early dawn of tax consciousness is debatable. But whatever the reasons, the phenomenon is not encouraging and does not suggest that we can run our economy without vigorous incentives.

INCENTIVES TO SAVE

Labor and management performance is not the only place where we must look for the effects of incentives. Savers, too, are human and subject to inducements. But if we think of the rate of interest as a method of stimulating more savings, we may be in for the same disappointment that we suffered in connection with higher wage rates and the willingness to work. The saver is delighted with a higher interest rate, but he does not necessarily save more in response. If he wants to buy a given amount of insurance, or is saving up for an annuity, he can have this for a smaller annual payment and may save a smaller part of his income rather than a larger one. People differently disposed may feel that with good bonds yielding 5 per cent it pays to put money away when at 2½ per cent it does not. In the longer run, a climate of capital scarcity, of which high interest rates would stand as a symbol, might invigorate the propensity to save. All things considered, including the restraint that high interest rates may exert on consumer credit, and on corporate willingness to forego retained profits in favor of higher dividend payments, the net effect of higher rates probably points toward more saving. But this is no very bright feather in the cap of the incentive doctrine.

What is true of interest rates applies also to taxes. We can not be sure that when the net return from savings is lowered by an income tax, savers will retaliate by saving less. A high income tax, it is true, makes it harder for the taxpayer to save because it takes more of his wherewithal. That, however, is an important but quite different matter. But the cut in the net return from savings, thanks to the tax, may make the saver jump either way.

The next step is to investigate how the saver invests the money the tax collector has left him. When taxes first went up sharply during the thirties, the popular doctrine was (and has remained to this day) that taxes discourage investment. This was asserted on behalf of savers' investment in securities as well as of business investment in plant and equipment. Eventually, economists discovered that the tax laws permit an offsetting of losses against profits. The chances of gain and loss, therefore, were not modified by the tax. The stakes simply became smaller.

Subsequent researches developed, however, that investors did not always respond to Uncle Sam's offer to share the loss as they should. Many investors, both those investing in securities and those investing in plant and equipment, seemed to concentrate rather singlemindedly on the profit prospects of the operation. If these were made unsatisfactory by the tax, they withdrew from the venture. Besides, the loss offset frequently proved a good deal less than perfect.

Nevertheless, numerous cases were found where the tax led to more, or more risky, investment. Particularly among individual investors, researchers discovered two broad groups: one leaning toward safety, another interested primarily in capital gains. The former were driven by the tax toward the shelter of ever safer investments. The latter, were pushed into assuming greater risk—as income became harder to earn, or at least to keep, capital gains increasingly looked like the only way to make real money.

Finally, the researchers discovered to their surprise that the creation of new businesses did not decline as a result of high taxes. The prospect of converting income into capital gains, by owning one's business, seems to have encouraged numerous bold spirits to strike out for themselves. Of course this finding applies only to the psychological side of the tax—the struggle between incentives and disincentives. It does not deny the chilling influence of taxes upon the young firm's ability to expand out of retained earnings.

~*~

Free Enterprise as a Gamble

So FAR, these are the findings of theorists and survey experts on the difficult subject of incentives. It is perhaps not unfair to them to say that to some extent they have left the matter where they found it—in a state of doubt. The evidence they uncovered suggests that incentives are important. It does not really tell us whether they are decisive.

MAN AGAINST THE ODDS

Perhaps we can throw some further light upon the working of the incentive system by reminding ourselves that the risk-taking it involves has an analogy with gambling. Some incentives offer cash on the barrel head, for instance when overtime is paid for extra work. Other incentives are more in the nature of pie in the sky. They offer an opportunity, a chance, but no guarantee. Often the odds are long, but if the reward is high, the lure may be strong.

This battle against odds can be fought in all walks of life. The investor takes up its challenge when he stakes his money on an unproven venture. The man who stakes his time and effort does the same. Wherever men set their sights toward high and distant goals—be it in business, in the professions or in government—they are gambling against odds. They may be risking their money, or they may be risking their time, health, family life and peace of mind by staking it on a career. They can never be certain of success, and in this sense they are gambling.

Gambling in the raw is not highly regarded by our society. In the words of Ambrose Bierce, "the gambling called business looks with austere disapproval upon the business called gambling." We disapprove of getting money for nothing, and even more of getting nothing for our money. But the type of gamble that consists in setting one's sights high is absolved and rightly so. The gamble is on the gambler's own ability to make the grade, and so the curse is taken from it.

Our moral predilections may tempt us to close our eyes to the gambling element, and to pretend that success is the certain reward of merit. In truth, the man who bets on his own ability can never be sure that he will outpace his competitors. Our sense of justice, our desire to see the best man win, leads us to overstress the admixture of merit and underrate the element of circumstance that turns the risk into a success. The race is not always to the swift nor the battle to the strong, although, as has been observed, that is the way to bet. Those who enter into a competition can be beaten not only by a better man but also by worse luck. Reward is uncertain; that is the essence of the incentive system.

The decision to take a chance—perhaps better, to take a bigger or smaller chance—faces the ambitious man at each stage of his education and career. After he has absorbed the legal minimum of schooling, ought he to go on to a higher education, if it means sacrifices? Will it pay off, in money and satisfactions? After he graduates, should he take a safe and well paid job with slow promotion in a big firm, or one at lower pay with some small aggressive outfit, where chances of triumph and disaster are equally immediate? Once he is launched in a job, should he try to get ahead or just to get along? Should he strike out for himself, start a new business? Should he risk his savings or keep them in the bank?

For the great bulk of people these decisions may be fairly automatic. Once they are made, it may not be easy to break out of the rut. Seniority, union rules, the speed of the assembly line, the anonymity of mass production raise formidable obstacles to individual achievement. Yet the chance is always there.

But although potentially the challenge is open to all, only a minority accept it. Of these, only a much smaller minority win through to the big prizes. The rest must accept partial success—a pessimist might call it partial failure. They may say quite honestly that they would do it all over again if they had to. Yet, if a young man with a vice-presidential dream could know in advance that he would end up as assistant branch manager, would he run quite so hard?

The willingness of men to accept a challenge of this sort is influenced by the size of the prizes and by the odds. We know quite a bit about the psychology of gambling. Where the stakes are small, most people (if they gamble) would be satisfied with a prize that does not cover the odds. A man may bet $2 at odds of 1:10 in order to win perhaps $17, although $20 would be required for an even break. But he will hardly, unless very rich, raise this bet to $2,000. To bet $2,000 at 1:10

odds, if at all, he would require a prize well above $20,000. More likely, he would prefer a much smaller prize, say $250, with the odds 10:1 in his favor, plus his money back.

The psychology is not hard to fathom. In the $2 bet the pleasure of gambling outweighs the small cost, and inadequate odds are made acceptable. This happens a million times a day, at race tracks, in bookie and numbers shops, in lotteries. When the ante is raised, the gambler is brought back to rationality. The $20,000 he might win will not, in most cases, be worth to him 10 times the $2,000 he risks—unless he is so rich that neither amount means much to him. It would take more than $20,000 to bring his subjective equation into balance. The wildcat oil well, drilled by a man of less than Texan format, may serve as an example. The $2,000 bet placed to earn $250 at odds of 10:1 in favor of the bettor, on the other hand, conforms broadly to the risks taken in a conservative common stock investment.

Most games of chance are not so simple, of course, and neither are the gambles of real life. Usually the alternatives are not to win or lose a fixed amount at fixed odds. Varying amounts at different and usually incalculable odds are at stake. A lottery, with its selection of small and big prizes, illustrates the principle. In business, total loss of investment and utter failure of career are less frequent than an unsatisfactory return and mediocre advancement.

Here, too, the conductors of lotteries and the operators of football pools can tell us something about the psychology of gambling, at least where moderate stakes are at issue. The uninitiated might think that the betting public would be indifferent as between a chance of, let us say, one in a million to make a million, and ten in a million to make 100,000. By no means so. Not long ago in Puerto Rico a socially conscious

Secretary of the Treasury decided to engage in some "income redistribution" among the potential winners in the government lottery. He cut the big prize, and increased the number of smaller ones. The total prize money remained unchanged. Sales of lottery tickets fell off promptly. The public preferred the smaller chance on the bigger prize. Football pools, with their enormous winnings, are organized on the same principle. Imagination evidently is kindled by the fabulous prize more than reason is chilled by the calculus of probability.

HOW TO ORGANIZE LIFE'S LOTTERY

What, if anything, do these observations tell us about how to organize the chances of economic life? Making allowances for the obvious differences, the interpretation of business and career as partial gamble suggest that there ought to be reasonably attractive prizes. A successful man gets paid not only for what he does. He gets paid also for doing it at the risk of not getting paid, or not getting paid adequately. A great many more people are left in just that position. They may have worked hard at their jobs to put themselves in line for a better one that ended up going to someone else. They may have explored some dead alley or come up with something good but not good enough. They tried, tried again till at last they failed. From them society gets more than it gives. They probably would not have done it without the chance for the pot of gold at the end of the rainbow.

The experience of the lottery also suggests that a few of the prizes should be on the rich side. It may seem a waste to let a man earn millions for something he would have been glad to do, on a contract basis, for a small fraction. Yet a few bonanzas seem to attract many who would not join the rush if rewards were less generous though more frequent. A few high prizes may be the best way of economizing on prize money.

Still another lesson of gambling, and an important one, is that most people don't like to gamble. Whether from rational appraisal of the chances, from lack of self-confidence, or from fear, the majority prefers security. The bondholders and job-holders of life outnumber the gamblers and venturers.

There is much to be said for their attitude. Only about 1 ½ per cent of all consumer units in the United States manage to earn over $25,000, only 5 per cent over $15,000. Of ten new businesses, five end within two years, eight within ten years, though by no means all of these terminations mean failure. The chances, statistically, of being even moderately success-ful are not overwhelming for the average person. Those who, having succeeded themselves, urge others to try usually great-ly underestimate the difficulties. One cannot blame men for not wanting to battle odds like these.

The economy must adjust itself to the needs of this group. It is, after all, the one that predominates. The economy must provide enough undramatic but safe jobs, careers and invest-ments. By failing to do so, it runs the risk of producing posi-tively harmful reactions, quite aside from questions of social justice. A sense of insecurity, a fear of unemployment, for instance, has often led to reduced efficiency through work stretching. Wildcat banking leads to banking in socks and under mattresses. Perhaps, once the members of the unad-venturous group feel a safe base under their feet, they will also be more inclined to respond to incentives that involve risk.

If this caveat is attended to, we can at least tell ourselves that the incentive economy is not grossly unfair to a majority of its members. It remains then to ask ourselves whether it is effective. How good a way is it of creating and improving the supply of goods and services?

The answer plainly must turn upon the small but venturesome segment of the population. If they are numerous—though still only a small per cent of the total—if they respond strongly to incentives, the economy will be far better than if they are few and timid. If they are timid, they will demand favorable odds for their ventures. As a group, they would then get a positive reward for their services, and this reward might have to be large. If they are exceptionally bold, they might be willing to take on odds that give them less than an even break. As a group, they would then end up with a deficit, compared with what it would cost to have their services on a contract basis instead of at a contingency fee. Society would be the gainer, most of the venturers the losers.

The venturers may be disappointed, in the aggregate, for still another reason. Even if they are determined to gamble only on favorable odds, they may miscalculate their chances. In a mixed game of chance and skill, it would not be surprising if healthy, confident men overestimated their potentialities. It is the essence of confidence not to be easily persuaded by adverse experience. If the participants in the game were polled, it might well turn out that 50 per cent of them expect to end up among the top 10 per cent. If so, they would be working under odds much more adverse than they think.

Official statistics do not deal in fanciful figures like these. Hence they throw little light on the question. If we look at the returns to business enterprise, we find that in 1959 they ran to not quite $60 billion. This looks like a pretty good return to venturing. But from this we would have to deduct taxes on personal income, and we would also have to deduct a charge for interest on the capital employed, before arriving at true profits. We would also have to allow for the going wage to proprietors. Calculations of this sort cannot respectably be put into print. Those I have made privately lead me to think that business men and stockholders do get a net profit for their venturing, though perhaps not a large one.

As far as career men are concerned, the matter is even more obscure. How much work is done in the hope of promotion by people who do not get promoted? How much is paid to men who do get promoted over and above the minimum they would have to get to do the kind of work they do? In a competitive society like ours, it is quite conceivable that society gets the best efforts of many people for less than they would cost on a contract basis. For every man who is appointed to a better job there is always at least one, usually more, who are disappointed. But we cannot say anything definite.

ABOLISH THE LOTTERY?

My views about the effects of the venturing system are essentially optimistic. This is a matter of opinion. But I do not want to leave the topic without considering the implications of a moderately pessimistic view. Suppose that even the bolder group demanded very substantial compensation for running risks—instead of being willing to pay for being allowed to venture, they would want to be paid highly for doing it. This may well be the actual situation. Would it mean that the system was bad? I think not—unless the compensation demanded was quite exorbitant.

It is true that society, faced with the need to pay its members for venturing, might be tempted to abolish this form of gambling. It might decide to terminate the gambling known as private enterprise. That would be socialism. But would it thereby remove the essential uncertainties of economic life that compel business men to take risks? Very likely not.

Whether an invention can be made commercial, whether a product will catch on, whether an investment will pay off, the socialist state knows no better than the capitalist business man. The socialist state can make its product a success by blocking all alternatives. In that case, neither the product nor its process of manufacture will probably be as good as if both had gone through a competitive process of trial and error. Whether the saving would be worth the drawbacks is at least debatable. The issue between socialism and capitalism will hardly be decided on this score. The point to be made is simply that if society must pay business men to undertake gambles, it gets something in return for the cost.

Neither can society hope to gain an obvious advantage by stopping the gamble inherent in the pursuit of a career. A completely aristocratic society might try it, at its peril. It might say to a young man, with A. A. Milne:

> We had intended you to be
> The next Prime Minister but three . . .

and so down the line for every job. It could then probably pay lower salaries to all those who had their careers guaranteed from oath of office to testimonial retirement dinner.

Whatever the merits of such a personnel policy, it would scarcely make for selection of efficient executives. No socialist society in its senses would try it. Neither would we.

⁄⁄∽⁄⁄

A Policy for Incentives

THE evidence about the role of incentives is now in. We have looked at the facts and at economic doctrine, we have also engaged in some rather fanciful speculations. What does it add up to?

THE CASE FOR INCENTIVES

There need be no argument over the critical role of human initiative and effort. An economic system cannot perform better than the people in it. Unanimity is less likely as to what can and should be done to create or safeguard economic incentives. It would surely be a mistake to make economic incentives the alpha and omega of policy. The economic motive, after all, is only one of many forces driving us, and we cannot even assume that it is the strongest. Economic incentives, moreover, appeal principally to a minority, even though entry into the economic race is open to all. Many in our society would have lost even before the start if their fate depended wholly on their ability to compete. A great many others, perhaps a majority, may have no great taste for the highly competitive life. They may respond to overtime pay, to the subtle temptations of incentive goods, to the warming stimulus of good human relations. But they would not be happy in a world of sink or swim, and might even respond negatively to intensely competitive incentives.

All this clearly seems to rule out, on ethical grounds alone, an economic system organized purely with a view to strengthening incentives. Laissez faire, survival of the fittest, rugged individualism in the sense of "devil take the hindmost," cannot be defended. Quite likely, moreover, they are not even the most effective kind of incentive system.

A system with more moderate incentives, such as ours at present, has proved itself to be quite effective. Social security has not led to widespread sloth. High taxes, which erode high incomes, have been found to erode the will to work in no comparable degree—at least for the time being. The performance of the American economy confirms this diagnosis. Staggering under the burden of a supposedly intolerable tax load, the economy has gone forward in the longest sustained advance of the present century. We might have done even better with lower taxes, but we cannot say we have done badly.

All this, I believe, can fairly be said in reply to extreme claims on behalf of the incentive system. But a good deal of solid substance remains. Until we succeed in turning the world into a bed of roses, an economic system can be too soft as well as too hard. If, at moderate cost, we can maintain and perhaps even strengthen our incentives without making life harder for those who do not respond, we shall probably have a better economy and a better life for everybody.

THE EGALITARIAN TREND

Belief in incentives is not a view which commands universal acceptance. There are many who think that the prizes held out by our economy are too generous, and would like to see them cut down. In part, their belief seems to reflect a more sceptical view of the effectiveness of such generosity. But this is scarcely the whole of the matter. It takes no great daring to conjecture the second root of these feelings: a deep-seated belief that large incomes are somehow unfair, immoral, or otherwise socially undesirable. Money makes its owner popular with those who have access to him, but unpopular with those who do not. Great wealth and high incomes have always been attacked, on grounds as often highminded as not. If these sentiments have abated somewhat since the days of the Great Depression and the war, the high income tax rates to which they gave birth have not.

This rise of egalitarian sentiment seems to me a greater threat to the incentive system than are the tax rates which it brings about. It threatens to remove the stamp of approval that still attaches to financial success. What to the Calvinists of old was evidence of divine blessing today becomes a source of popular irritation. Since the upper income brackets talk mostly to each other (this has been held to be one of the penalties of being rich), they probably do not feel this too strongly. But in the long run they cannot help sensing the change in climate, and reacting to it. We have seen how, in some European circles after the war, "profit" became a wicked word. The United States itself barely escaped this fixation during the depression.

Some of that feeling undoubtedly is still in the air. It clearly has influenced what business men say, if not what they do. If it grows, it will affect action as well as speech. Fewer able young men will go into business. Those who go will be less single minded in their activities. Perhaps that would be a good thing, in some respects. But it would cramp the incentive system.

The egalitarians will reply, of course, that there are other forms of excelling than by making money, and other incentives than the purely economic. I fear they misunderstand their own crusade. Today they battle inequalities of income and wealth because those are the most obvious and important ones in our society. But if they succeed, and if emulation and invidious comparison manifest themselves in some other field—power, prestige, universal pulling of rank—will they rest?

Those who know the egalitarians and usually value their friendship doubt it. Egalitarians must equalize, and so are driven to oppose all forms of inequality. Ultimately this means to oppose all rewards of achievement. Perhaps achievement itself may survive, as its own reward. But is not achievement, too, an invidious distinction? The final result of a program to abolish inequalities and distinctions might well be to make achievement itself odious. To compete aggressively, to press ahead, to push others into the background might become bad taste. Individual success might develop an unethical flavor. Teamwork and cooperation might altogether displace individual initiative and competition.

Something of this sort is already happening in a gentlemanly way. Books like Riesman's *The Lonely Crowd* and Whyte's *The Organization Man* describe it dramatically. "Other-directed" man, acutely aware of the reactions of the people around him, is replacing "inner-directed" man, who was guided mainly by his own convictions, desires, complexes. "Antagonistic cooperation" among members of management teams takes the place of old-fashioned competition. And the hard-hitting drive toward the top is displaced by the relaxed approach to a middle stratum, well protected from the blasts that sweep the icy peaks. The ultimate stigmatization of achievement is not a futuristic nightmare. It is beginning to happen even while we talk blithely about whether to strengthen incentives or not.

This change of climate, not the level of taxes, poses the

real threat. Taxes may press on incentives, here and there, and do some damage. So long as non-financial incentives remain alive, taxes will not drive initiative and achievement out of business. But when our social mores begin to turn against the man who stands out, we are up against something new and incalculable. When good performance becomes bad manners, incentives cease to bite and the mainspring of action goes dead. Uneconomic man in the disincentive economy stands at the end of this evolution.

We are under no obligation to join in this trend. We may continue to prefer Riesman's "inner-directed" individualist to the "other-directed" cooperator and to do what we can to keep the window open to fresher breezes against the grey flannel climate indoors. To those who are not social determinists, there is nothing inevitable about the present drift. Our social diagnosticians, the discoverers of what might be called "Riesman's disease," do not say that the ailment has no cure. What will happen depends in good part on how we feel about it, and what we are going to do about it. The plea for strong incentives becomes, in this context, a plea also for a less conformist, more spontaneous, form of existence.

These incentives—this bears repeating—cannot be of the sink-or-swim type. Extreme penalties for poor performance are out of keeping with the times, even if their true effectiveness were not suspect. Insofar as possible, rewards must be used instead of penalties. The carrot must replace the stick. Intangible incentives are preferable to purely economic. Rewards, whenever possible, should be non-material—but not immaterial. With these signposts clearly marked, we need not be embarassed even in this age of lonely crowds to argue for a system of vigorous incentives.

IV

EQUALITY

In the United States of America, in the year of prosperity
1957, some 5 per cent of the consumer units collected 20 per
cent of total personal income. At the other end of the scale,
20 per cent had to make do with 5 per cent. Per consumer
unit, the prosperous 5 per cent at the top had sixteen times more
than their less successful countrymen at the bottom. These
hard facts call for some hard thinking.

We have made great strides in our country toward political
equality, and we have made a good advance also toward a class-
less society. Practically nobody in the United States thinks of
himself as belonging to "the proletariat." It takes a sociologist
with a research grant to discover an American aristocrat.
How, then, do we reconcile economic inequality with our
belief in political equality? If one man rates one soul and
one vote, why should he be worth widely varying amounts
of dollars?

For a partial answer, we can truthfully say that the real
differences are not so big as they look in the *Statistical Abstract
of the United States*. Figures don't lie, but they may distort.
It can be pointed out, for instance, that the gap in living
standards is much smaller than the gap in incomes. It is smaller,
too, than the rich-poor gap in most other countries. And the
living standards of even the lowest group in the United States
are still well above the average standard of most of the people

on the globe. The width of the rich-poor gap, moreover, has been shrinking during most of the industrial period, despite what many people seem to believe.

Yet the fact remains that the logic of our economic system demands some degree of economic inequality, even in the face of the egalitarianism of our political system. We have argued the need for economic incentives in the previous chapter. Incentives, if they work, mean that some men will earn more than others. We must now face up to the consequences of those recommendations. What have we let ourselves in for?

First of all, we shall have to establish some brief facts about income inequality in the United States. These will enable us to see the problem in its proper perspective. Next, we shall have to ask ourselves how much of this inequality can be justified, in the light of our moral beliefs as well as of any practical benefits it may bring. The old problem of the morality and usefulness of private property cannot be side-stepped here. Finally, we must consider one kind of equality that is vital to a healthy capitalism: that of opportunity.

ഌ

Facts

THE statistics of income distribution turned out by the Department of Commerce are a product of many-sided usefulness. They serve social reformers in arousing moral indignation, advertising agencies in conducting market research, and last but not necessarily least, economists in their efforts to understand the economy. Table I below shows the number of families in different income brackets (before taxes), from the humble "under $2000" to the majestic "$50,000 and over," and the same for unattached individuals. "Income" here follows the national income concept and includes "imputed" income, such as rental value of homes occupied by their owners, and food consumed by the farmer from his own farm. Statistics of "money income" only, which are frequently bandied about, can make the United States look extremely poor. In 1958, they put 7 per cent of all spending units below $1000, 20 per cent below $2000.[1] Aside from their capacity to muddle issues, they are of limited usefulness.

TABLE I
INCOMES IN THE UNITED STATES, 1957

Family Personal Income before Income Taxes	Families Number (thousands)	Per Cent	Unattached Individuals Number (thousands)	Per Cent
Under $2,000	3,589	8.2	4,075	40.8
$2,000–$2,999	3,289	7.5	2,106	21.1
$3,000–$3,999	4,879	11.2	1,614	16.2
$4,000–$4,999	5,869	13.4	975	9.8
$5,000–$5,999	5,653	12.9	539	5.4
$6,000–$7,499	7,204	16.5	321	3.2
$7,500–$9,999	6,581	15.1	192	1.9
$10,000–$14,999	4,195	9.6	94	.9
$15,000–$19,999	1,256	2.9	25	.3
$20,000–$24,999	477	1.1	12	.1
$25,000–$49,999	538	1.2	20	.2
$50,000 and over	140	.3	7	.1
Total	43,670	100.0	9,980	100.0

Source: U. S. Department of Commerce, *Survey of Current Business,* April 1960.

THE RICH AND THE POOR

The real meat of Table I is to be found around the middle brackets. Here we see how the great bulk of the people split up the bulk of the income. Into these brackets fall the happy mean incomes of $6,975 for families and of $2,930 for unattached individuals, figures of some impressiveness.

But the drama comes, of course, at the extremes. Some 140,000 families and 7,000 highly eligible unattached individuals enjoyed incomes in excess of $50,000; their average income was $85,712. At the bottom, 3,589,000 families and 4,075,000 unattached individuals failed to make more than $2,000; on average they eked out only $1,124. These make up the unenviable category of low income receivers which often is quoted as a prime exhibit against the American economy.

We shall presently discover that the degree of inequality is not as bad as it looks, though still distressing enough. First, however, we shall have to make certain emendations to the figures that will make some of them look worse. The top brackets, high as they tower, are still understated, because they do not allow for unrealized capital gains. Capital gains may result from undistributed corporate profits, reflected in the price of stocks, or from any of the many rational and irrational elements that influence the minds of investors and the price of their assets. In any case, capital gains are the principal source of wealth in an age when it is no longer possible to get very rich by saving out of even a multi-hundred thousand dollar income. If unrealized capital gains could be added to the earned incomes of the upper brackets they would —in years of rising markets—make some spectacular reading. The bottom brackets, too, stand in need of corrections and here the corrections do make more pleasant reading. First of all, many of the inhabitants of the lowest bracket are transients rather than permanent residents. People enter and leave the labor force, families are formed and dissolved, people leave their jobs and advance in their careers. Each month about three and a quarter million people enter the labor force, and not quite the same number leave it. That makes for a large number of part-year incomes. A college graduate starting on a $3,600 job after commencement gets into the less than $2,000 bracket for that year. This kind of thing accounts for many "low incomes." A distribution by "lifetime incomes" would redress these distortions and so would be more meaningful. It would also bring down many families from the upper brackets into which they were catapulted by temporary success.

Capital consumption by old people contributes a second practical explanation of the "low income" situation. An investment of $50,000 in high-grade bonds may yield less than $2,000, but between income and principal it can provide not too badly for a retired couple. Third, the cost of living varies surprisingly within the United States. It is hardly necessary to observe that if one has to live on $2,000 a year, he will be less uncomfortable in a rural than in an urban environment. Finally, the low income families have the relative advantage of being smaller. Close to one-half of them consist of only two people. That an income below $2,000 does not in all cases signify penury is suggested by the frequency of home ownership in this group. It runs to 45 per cent among urban, and to more among rural families, and it about equals the rate of home ownership among families with incomes of $2,000 to $4,000. More low income families own their homes free of mortgage than do the moderate income families, no doubt owing to their higher family age.

But when all is done that should be to set straight the lower bracket statistics, a serious indictment nevertheless remains. Many hundreds of thousands of families permanently live on incomes that are far less than adequate for a wholesome existence. Is this the inevitable fruit of inequality? Can these pockets of poverty be cleaned out without a major redistribution of income?

A closer look at the people caught in these pockets tells us that wholesale redistribution is probably not the answer. They are there not as a class but as individuals, brought there by some identifiable condition. Lack of education and job training of the family head has been found a frequent feature of low income families. Broken homes are another. Advanced age frequently enters as an aggravating or sometimes even sole cause. Certain regions, especially in the South, account for a disproportionate share of low income families.

These causes of low income and earning power can and must be attacked on their own grounds. Soaking the rich is no assured way of removing ignorance, mending family ties, providing for old age, or improving regional economies. All such undertakings demand money, hence taxes, but what they require far more and more urgently is energetic private and public action. We have reduced poverty to a hard core, and continued growth will no doubt continue to chip away at it. But in its present state, the evil plainly is more social than economic. It is less a matter of general inequality of income than of particular difficulties and misfortunes. It will have to be met on those terms.

THE DIMINISHING IMPORTANCE OF INEQUALITY

The ultimate conquest of poverty is still ahead of us. This major achievement of American civilization, though 90 per cent completed, still demands a final push. But by removing poverty as far as we did, we also have, almost without noticing it, done away with much of the earlier inequality.

As late as 1929, for instance, the top 5 per cent of all families (excluding single individuals) received 31 per cent of total personal income. By 1950 their share had dropped to 20 per cent—both figures taken before income taxes, which would further cut down the share particularly in 1950. The share of the top 20 per cent, before taxes, dropped from 55 per cent to 44 per cent over the same span. Meanwhile, the share of the lower 40 per cent went up from 13½ per cent to 18 per cent, without counting government contributions, which would raise the 1950 share of this group.[2]

Some discounts for statistical ambiguities must be allowed for. If corporate profits—including those taxed away—are added to the income of the upper groups, the progress of equalization becomes less striking. It would become even less striking if lifetime instead of annual incomes were studied, because in that case the inequality of 1929 would appear less marked. But in their broad sweep, the data suggest that pre-tax inequality has been cut back in some substantial degree, even without considering what taxes and public benefits have accomplished in the way of redistribution.

What forces are behind this deconcentration of incomes? Fundamentally, the constant change and infinite variety of American society is responsible. Property changes hands and changes in value, self-made men displace old families, industries flourish and decay, labor moves from farm to the city and from job to better job, political forces break down vested interests. All this means rotation in top brackets—few families stay there permanently. It also means dispersal and equalization of wealth and income. Whoever first said, "From shirt-sleeves to shirtsleeves in three generations"—whether he was an admirer or a critic of American society—pointed, with pardonable exaggeration, to something very real. This something—the dynamics of America—first created great concentrated wealth. Now it has begun to even things up again.

The fundamental forces have been aided generously by the fisc. Over and beyond the equalization of incomes before taxes and transfer payments, further leveling has been accomplished by a progressive tax structure, and by public services in cash and in kind, aimed chiefly at the lower income groups. The top 5 per cent has felt the principal weight of this taxation: Their share, *after* taxes, had dropped from 29 per cent during the 1920's to 18 per cent in 1946. How much the citizenry in general, at all levels of the income scale, has been lowered or raised by redistribution can only be conjectured.

The last of the leveling forces has been our rising standard of living itself. During the nineteenth century, the lives of a well-to-do family and of a working man exhibited some marked differences. These differences have been shrinking rapidly, even between families whose dollar incomes are as far apart as ever. The rising standard of living in the lower brackets has made servants a vanishing species. It has in effect closed the large old homes and compelled all but the really rich to find more manageable quarters. Today the majority of families throughout the income scale have homes of their own, some homes smaller than others but few totally different. All kinds of homes depend on the same household appliances, and their owners drive cars that differ in price but often in no other visible feature. The families watch the same TV programs on sets of moderately different size. The $25,000 family enjoys a variety of extras, but its basic form of living is not very obviously distinguishable from that of the $6,000 family. With higher incomes yielding no radically different forms of living, it is surprising that incentives have not, apparently, suffered commensurately.

To finish with the facts of economic inequality in America: They seem to be a good deal less grim than critics try to make believe. That is the principal conclusion to be extracted from the data. Strong forces are at work to soften them as time passes, even without benefit of redistributive taxation. What remains as our principal problem is sporadic poverty produced mainly by individual circumstances. These are not readily amenable to general equalization; they demand direct attack. Inequality as an issue is losing much of its drawing power.

~∞~

The Morals of Inequality

OUR survey of the facts has shown that there is probably less to economic inequality than meets the eye. Nevertheless, there is still enough to make one uneasy and to compel one to search for either remedy or justification.

This reaction, which seems to come naturally in an egalitarian country, would not have come at all times and places. History knows many civilizations that were built on an unquestioning acceptance of inequality, political as well as economic. The glory of Greece and the grandeur of Rome were built on slavery. Plato's philosophy of government rejected equality in favor of a rigid hierarchy of classes. The teachings of the Church during the Middle Ages and its contemporary feudal society took inequality on earth as given by God and pleasing to Him. Our sensitivity to the problems of inequality is of surprisingly recent date.

This sensitivity to the injustice of unequal incomes varies not only in time, but also in space. Some European countries today seem to be more "sicklied o'er with the pale cast of thought" than the United States. But wherever the question arises, one observes two extremes between which the great majority find their places: Those who see nothing wrong with the existing distribution of incomes, or one even more unequal, and those who take for granted that the only fair shares are equal shares. Each side has its arguments to demonstrate that its position is "naturally just."

Those who approve of inequality usually point to the obvious facts of life. Human beings are biologically unequal. The equality that the Constitution speaks of is one of rights, not of condition—before God and the law, not in the market place. The basic truth of these propositions is undeniable, even though the readiness of their proponents to bear other people's poverty with fortitude is sometimes a little irritating. Yet perhaps not much is proved by truths such as these. If man is the master of his fate, why should he not correct the consequences of biological inequality if he finds them unattractive? We have gone some way in evening up what nature made uneven—why not go the whole way?

The supporters of inequality are fond also of saying that, after all, anybody can get rich if he tries hard enough; this is a free country and those who remain poor have only themselves to blame. That is true enough in any particular case— leaving aside the question of whether the "case" has the ability to work his way to the top. It is conspicuously fallacious for the people as a whole. Even if the population of the United States consisted exclusively of men with the ability and determination of Rockefeller, Ford and Carnegie, they could not all be presidents of corporations. Circumstances—luck, connections and whatever—must inevitably lead a few to the top and keep the vast majority in the lower echelons. We cannot all get ahead of one another.

Finally, one often hears it said in support of income inequality that, after all, a man has a right to the fruits of his labor. If he is smart enough to make a million, why should he not be entitled to it? Those who say this are speaking, although they may not always remember it, in a distinguished tradition, that of John Locke. The English philosopher rested his defense of private property upon the grounds that property was, in the last analysis, something acquired through labor, and that everyone had a right to what he produced. This principle carried conviction in the days when craftsmen and farmers really "made" what they lived by. Today it does not speak to us quite so clearly. When a man "makes" a million in business today, what is it he really makes, and how much of it is his own contribution? How much is contributed by his collaborators, his predecessors, by society at large? How much of it depends on the state of competition, the state of business and a host of other factors not demonstrably under his control? Economists believe that, under favorable conditions, they can calculate the contribution that an individual makes to the flow of production with the help of the marginal productivity doctrine. But they rarely have the courage to extract a moral claim from such calculations.

If those who regard economic inequality as "natural" fail to make a convincing case, those who go for equality as "the only just solution" perform no better. Righteous indignation and vicarious anguish at the sight of poverty do not add up to a logical demonstration. Equality of income as a principle of justice runs straight into the fact that men are unequal not only as producers but also as consumers. Some of us want an expensive education, some want to travel, some want great variety in clothes, living habits and entertainment—others may find all of this tiresome. Temperaments, moreover, may vary as well as tastes—we were created equal, but not equally cheerful. To endow everybody with equal income will certainly make for very unequal enjoyment and satisfaction. Perhaps some sort of allowance could be made for this. But in practice it would scarcely be feasible to determine for purposes of compensation how many drinks above or below par each individual happened to be born.

The plea for equality also offends the elementary feeling that there should be some relation between performance and reward. We cannot say, to be sure, that a man has a right to whatever he makes, because today there are few things of which we can say who really "made" them. Yet to say positively that a man has no right to what he makes seems to imply that someone else has a better right, which makes little sense. The right of any member of society to an equal share, moreover, would presumably depend on his having put forth a normal amount of effort. To hand a full share to those who not only do not succeed, but do not even try, will strike most people as perverse. Justice seems to escape the egalitarians as it has evaded those who believe in "natural" differences.

⚘

What Sort of Inequality?

PART of this debate amounts to no more than a conflict between self-interest and sentimentality. But it has an honest core, and the wide differences that it reveals among men of good will point to a conflict deeper than pocketbook interest. This conflict can be pursued all the way up into the family history of our term "equality." Among the three sister virtues "liberty, equality, fraternity" which the French Revolution held before the world, "fraternity" originally possessed much of the emotional content today carried by equality. Equality, in turn, was closer to liberty—freedom from oppression and equal treatment under the law. But fraternity—probably too good for this world—early withdrew from public life. Equality, though a little dowdy and somewhat lacking in generosity, in part took her place. In her new and expanded guise she promptly fell out with her former ally, liberty: The compulsion to conform to uniform standards was discovered to be at odds with the right to be different. Early observers of American democracy, especially de Tocqueville, worried gloomily over this conflict. The "tyranny of the majority" was their phrase for the threat emanating from oppressive egalitarianism.

The conflict between freedom and equality has become deeper as equality increasingly has come to mean economic equality. By the same token, however, equality has lost a good part of its halo and much of the ready support that it formerly commanded. For looked at cold-bloodedly, what sort of an ideal is this economic equality? What claims to a fair minded man's allegiance does it have, what sense does it make as a goal?

Equality of rights before the law is intuitively appealing as a social goal. Particular individuals might of course want for themselves greater powers and privileges than equality of rights would allow. But it is clear that their desires could be granted only at the expense of someone else. The sum total of rights and powers in a community remains fixed—it adds up to 100 per cent. Any extra rights given to some mean extra obligations placed upon the rest. It is strictly a case of "the more there is of mine, the less there is of yours." In such a situation, equal sharing of rights and powers offers the obvious solution.

, This obvious solution does not translate smoothly into economics. Here the obvious goal seems to be, not equal welfare, but maximum welfare. A man can have more than others and yet not take anything from them, if he creates his own surplus. Economic equality as such seems to bestow no particular blessings. A community where some were rich and the rest well provided for presumably would be considered better off than one in which all were equally poor. Economic equality, unlike its political counterpart, plainly is not an end in itself. It is only a means, designed to reduce poverty; perhaps it is not the most effective means.

That economic equality does not rank with political equality as a moral ideal is plain on several grounds. To demand that none have privileges I do not enjoy seems fair. To insist that none be richer is merely spiteful. People's behavior, moreover, makes clear that economic equality is rarely their true goal. What they strive for is betterment. Insofar as they compare themselves with others, it seems that emulation, the creation of invidious distinctions, as Veblen has so well observed, turns out to be a stronger motive than desire for equality. Equality appears in the main as a steppingstone for the underdog on his way to becoming top dog. Once he is past the halfway mark, his interest in equality usually tends to abate. The successful self-made man characteristically seems to be far less concerned about the injustice of inequality than the man whose inheritance weighs heavily on his conscience. In matters of money, there are few who are prepared to say, as Walt Whitman did about democracy, "I will accept nothing that all cannot have on even terms."

I may have labored unnecessarily the simple conclusion that economic equality or inequality is not primarily a matter of justice. But to those who do not find the conclusion obvious, or obviously wrong, the argument may be of service. To speak against any form of equality, in our day and age, is uphill work. The climate of opinion and the doubts of his own conscience weigh heavily upon the speaker. Yet it seems clear that the debate over justice in distribution largely misses its point. The real issue is not which division, equal or unequal, is the more just. The issue is which of the two leads to higher welfare for all. The functional, rather than the moral, aspects of distribution are what matter, and it is these we will look at now.

வ௦ம

Inequality and Progress

IF WELFARE is our goal, equal sharing of incomes can claim to be the best road to it—provided we live in a static economy, incapable of growth. I shall shortly argue that a dynamic economy changes this fundamentally, that inequality promotes growth, and that growth is worth more than redistribution. Meanwhile, however, the neat logic of the welfare case for equality demands attention.

THE WELFARE CASE FOR EQUALITY

The case for greater equality can be established very simply. A dollar means less to a richer man than to a poorer. Therefore, if we take a dollar from the rich man and give it to the poor man, we hurt the rich man less than we help the poor. The sum total of their happiness rises by virtue of the operation. Happiness can be further increased by additional transfers and will reach its peak when everybody's income is up or down to the average and complete economic equality is achieved.

Scientific economics sees a fly in the egalitarian ointment. All we really know is that the millionth dollar means less than the thousandth *to the same man*. We cannot be sure that the millionth dollar means less to one man than the thousandth means to another. True enough, one of these men is rich, the other is poor. But perhaps the pauper is completely satisfied with what he has, while the millionaire is pressed for cash. Or perhaps the pauper is an insensitive clod, incapable of finer feelings, while the millionaire is a delicate aesthete who can exist only in complete luxury. More realistically, the millionaire is probably accustomed to his standard of living and the pauper to his. Even if they are fairly similar individuals, it may hurt the one more to cut his standard than it will cheer the other to increase his.

Rigorous economic theory, therefore, will not subscribe unqualifiedly to the egalitarians' doctrine that redistribution from rich to poor must increase total satisfaction. Nevertheless, for practical purposes, the case is pretty strong, the objections not very convincing. Individuals' differ, but people in the mass fall into fairly stable patterns. I would hate to have to argue that the members of the upper income brackets are on average more sensitive and capable of greater enjoyment than the rest. And the unquestionable hardships that would result from a reduction of the upper living standards could be softened by spreading the process over a generation or two.

Thus put, the case for equality is impressive, simply on functional grounds and aside from questions of justice. It can hardly fail to predispose us in favor of greater rather than lesser equality, whenever this does not interfere with growth, or boomerang in other respects. In fact, however, it is apt to defeat itself in these respects more often than not. That will be the next step of the argument.

GROWTH VS. REDISTRIBUTION

Once growth comes to be seen as an alternative to redistribution, its potential superiority in providing welfare becomes quickly apparent. Even those who are at the low end of the income scale stand to gain more, in the not-very-long run, from speedier progress than from redistribution. Redistribution is a one-shot operation. What it can do for the lower income groups amounts to less, as we have seen, than its enthusiasts claim. Soaking the rich yields political dividends, but not much consumable revenue. And once it is done, the toll of a lower rate of progress is exacted continually thereafter. If the rate of income growth in an egalitarian economy is 2 per cent per year, and 4 per cent in one allowing itself a higher degree of inequality, it will not be many years before the middle class of the egalitarian economy is outdistanced by the "poor" of the other.

The proposition that rapid progress is worth more than redistribution even to the poor has been challenged occasionally. The critics argue that the standard of poverty rises with the standard of living. Accordingly, if we succeeded in doubling or quadrupling the average standard of living, those who fell below it would feel just as poor as they do today. To redistribute, to raise the poor closer to the average, would thus be a surer road to happiness.

Even on their own gloomy premises, these critics overlook one obvious flaw in their reasoning: What happens to the man above the average? If the poor man feels poor simply because he is below average no matter how well off he really is, the rich man presumably feels rich because he is above average. If some future New Deal averages the poor up, it must average the rich down. The first gain, but the others lose.

What really demands our attention here, however, is the gloomy premise itself, which says that apparently we can never get ahead of our needs. This economic relativity theory is profoundly pessimistic—in fact it seems to put an end to all meaningful economic endeavor. No matter how rich we get, the doctrine says, no matter how equally we split our wealth, as a community we shall never feel any better off. We might as well stop working after lunch and cultivate our intellects.

There is probably more than a grain of truth in this doctrine. Man's capacity for enjoyment is limited, luxuries quickly become necessities, and money, as has been observed on occasion, is no guarantee of happiness. Material progress does not fill man's life—fortunately. But that is just one part of the story. If man is constitutionally unable, as these critics seem to think, to achieve happiness, he can at least do something to reduce the positive ills of this vale of tears. Schopenhauer argued that while pleasure is an illusion, pain is real. With all our high standard of living, we still have enough sources of pain—illness, unprotected old age and, above all, lack of real leisure. So long as these are with us, there is little point in even wondering whether or not we would be made happier by more and more progress.

Those who take the gloomy view of man's capacity for happiness must bear in mind, besides, that one answer to their problem can be found precisely in the rapid progress which they want to sacrifice for the joys of equality. It is true that the satisfactions of having and being pall in time. But getting and becoming are always fresh sensations. Insofar as material welfare and creature comforts can do anything for men at all, it is their increase, more than their level, that brings satisfaction. Here lies such justification as one may find for singing the perhaps debatable praises of progress.

CREATIVE INEQUALITY

Let us put aside now the question of whether economic inequality is inequitable. Instead, let us look more searchingly at its constructive role in the economy.

One important explanation of, and reason for, inequality follows from the need to get the right people into the right jobs. It is wasteful if engineers do work that mechanics can handle, or if executives perform chores that could be done by their secretaries. A market economy avoids this by compelling business to compete for talent and to pay each man what he is worth in the job he can do best. The process admittedly works far from perfectly. Many of our income differentials arise from monopoly power rather than from greater productivity. This is true of some wage rates and salaries higher up the line, as well as of some of the profits of venture capital. The benefits of inequality of this sort—except to the recipients—are questionable. But even in more perfect markets, large differentials would arise.

These differentials could be taxed away, of course, as in part they are today. The effectiveness of the selection process, however, suffers correspondingly. A high salary that one cannot keep is no great attraction. Unless we pay people what they are worth, they may see to it that they are worth no more than they are paid. Therefore, if the selection process results in large bonuses, efficiency demands that, in good part, they be left where they land.

Another instance of creative inequality presents itself when we turn to incentives. Here again, the logic of our system produces inequalities that cannot be removed without slowing down the system itself. If we want good performance, we must hold out rewards. To be effective, rewards must raise one man above the other. Not their absolute level, but their differentiation is what counts, as we discovered in the discussion of incentives. Inequality once more proves to be the price of progress and efficiency.

It might be possible, of course, to shift the needed inequalities from the economic sphere to that of status, prestige and power. In part—to the extent that economic differentials are taxed away—that shift is likely to come automatically, even though unofficially. We should then be moving into the world of Orwell's *Animal Farm*, where everybody is equal, but some are more equal than others. I see no reason to think that power and prestige differentials are any more "just" than economic ones. Certainly they could be a great deal more unpleasant.

If a thoroughgoing economic egalitarianism were to take hold, its chief victim probably would be the incentive to take risks. Successful risk-taking has built most of the big fortunes. It is here that the egalitarians would find their most inviting targets. It is here, also, that the conjunction between equality and stagnation might make itself felt most strongly.

The incentive to invest, to be sure, is not exclusively wedded to the profit motive. It is related to other motivations —competition, sheer expansionism, prestige—which were duly noted in the preceding chapter. But remove profit and enough of the motive force probably will be gone to slow down the rest.

The ability to save is another important consequence of high incomes that has often been stressed. The rich, as has been correctly observed, can afford to save a good part of their incomes. The poor, unfortunately, save little or nothing. Leveling of incomes, it has therefore been thought, would perforce reduce the rate of saving. This argument was especially popular during the Great Depression, when saving tended to outrun investment opportunities. A cut in saving and a corresponding rise in consumption would then have aided recovery. Redistribution of income would have killed two birds with one tax hike.

To the credit of those who developed this doctrine and derived from it a pleasure perhaps more than intellectual, it must be said that they were also the first to discover that the doctrine may not fit the statistical evidence. What they discovered from income distribution data and personal budget studies was rather surprising. A man with $10,000 a year net may save $1,000 and a man with $4,000 may save nothing. But out of any dollar added to their respective incomes, both may save sums that are not so very different. In other words, it is true that the upper brackets save more of their *total* income; it is somewhat doubtful that they save much more than the poor also out of an *increase* in income. A change in income —up or down—seems to lead to a fairly similar change in saving for upper and lower brackets alike.

If this is so, a redistribution of income from rich to poor would cause the poor to begin saving possibly as much as the rich would cease to save. Redistribution, on these premises, would not greatly change the volume of saving out of current income. It would not help to cure a depression brought on by over-saving. By the same token, it would not greatly cut into the savings needed by a fast growing, high employment economy. The statistical facts which deprived the liberals of a favorite argument for redistribution have robbed conservatives of an old war horse in the struggle against the egalitarians.

The statistical findings, however, are not entirely clear cut. In Jacob Viner's phrase, there may be life in the old dogma yet. And it can be further reinvigorated by stressing that it is not only the quantity but also the quality of savings that counts. Industry needs venture capital, and that is not usually supplied by insurance companies buying bonds nor even by pension funds buying blue chip stocks. Venture capital typically comes from wealthy individuals. To dry up their savings would still create an important gap in our financial structure, even though dollarwise they could be replaced from other sources. This much can fairly be argued by those who see a threat in equalization.

On the firing line against egalitarianism, we find also a belief, sometimes a little camouflaged, in the need for an elite —cultural, intellectual, political, economic. Stated in terms of a need for a privileged aristocracy, the view sounds offensive to American ears. The belief in the virtues of a leisure class, in particular, has taken a bad drubbing at the hands of Thorstein Veblen—in the one country where a leisure class proper has scarcely existed. But when the idea is reformulated in terms of "leadership," many people will probably be inclined to agree that something of this sort, based on merit, is needed. Most of the great achievements that history remembers or contemporaries admire are very clearly connected with the existence of a leadership group.

In a minor key, the need for leadership in consumption is

readily arguable. It becomes most obvious in very poor countries, where equality would allow none to rise much above subsistence. It may appear less convincing in a rich country like the United States. Nevertheless, our own experience shows the advantages, for instance, of consumer pioneering. We are all ready to keep up with the Joneses, provided there are Joneses to keep up with. Anyone will buy something that is a necessity, but someone first has to smooth its transition from luxury to the more humdrum status. Conspicuous consumption, in a country constantly offering new kinds of goods, is creative consumption. An egalitarian society promises to be virtuous, frugal and dull.

These ideas do not lend themselves to quantification. It is impossible to say how concentrated wealth should be to stimulate the creation of luxuries, and how well spread to speed up their conversion to mass necessities. To push the need for consumer pioneering very hard smacks unpleasantly of snobbism. But to reject the notion altogether would be evidence of the very egalitarian conformism against which it protests.

One further point deserves to be made. Economic inequality is not purely an economic affair. It touches also upon political stability and social cohesion. In an extreme case, inequality may lead to revolution. So may overzealous efforts to reduce it. A distribution of income that is widely resented may, even though it is economically efficient, do more political harm than economic good. A society that has got itself into this frame of mind will probably be wise to pay the economic price of its political idiosyncrasies. Slower progress would then have to be written off as the cost of political and social betterment.

Added to its probable price in terms of growth, action to alter the distribution of income determined by the market is likely to impose a non-economic cost. Typically, this cost takes the form of lengthening the reach of government. Something, somebody, has to be registered, regulated, controlled. A little freedom always goes by the board. Some economic resources, too, that could perhaps be more productively employed must be shifted to this function. If anyone thinks that this is altogether a negligible matter, let him note the lack of enthusiasm with which taxpayers vote the means for even the most pressing functions of government.

HOW MUCH INEQUALITY?

We may safely conclude that progress will come faster if some degree of inequality is tolerated. The right man must be put into the right job and given the right incentives. Savings must be kept flowing, and the taste for risk-taking kept alive. There must be scope for consumer pioneering. In addition, we can save ourselves some added regimentation if we are willing to push less hard for equality. All this supports the case for accepting a certain measure of inequality.

A certain measure—but how much? The range is wide, from literal and absolute equality to the equally implausible state of an Eastern potentate of the old days surrounded by a subsistence population. Neither condition commends itself as a base for progress.

Unfortunately, most of the considerations that argue against complete equality desert us when we want to know about the right degree of inequality. Only the market criterion has an answer. It says, in effect, "Put each man in the job which he does best, and pay him what he is worth in it." If we expand this idea to cover also the employment of peoples' savings— pay each type of capital, venturesome or timid or in between, what it produces in its proper use—we end up with a distribution of income according to the market's valuation.

But the market criterion is only one among several. If we judge the desirable degree of inequality according to the incentives that are needed, we may find that the market criterion overshoots the goal. A man may feel himself driven to do his best in response to a reward that would underpay him according to his market value. Why not tax away the difference?

The savings criterion, too, is tantalizingly unspecific. Would a strong concentration of income, if it tends toward higher saving, mean faster progress? It probably would, if that income is concentrated in the hands of an authoritarian government which channels into investment every cent above a low level of consumption. It would not lead to much progress, however, if the recipient were an oldstyle potentate surrounded by a population without purchasing power, without wants—in short, without a market.

The consumer pioneering criterion of inequality, finally, is likewise more emphatic than specific in its advice. What sort of inequality does it imply? The sort that enabled the Medicis to subsidize Renaissance art and literature? Or the kind that allows the Joneses to have a new portable grill ahead of the rest of us? In the absence of specific answers to such questions, the optimum inequality remains very much a matter of opinion, no matter how willing one may be to surrender equality as a goal in favor of growth.

CONCLUSION

The views presented so far can be summarized very simply. Those who think that we are in a stagnant state will find that to equalize incomes is not only just, but also functionally efficient. It would be the way to get the most out of a permanently circumscribed total.

Those who for some reason are little concerned about growth likewise will find that equalization fits their book. It can be counted upon to remove most of what makes for tension and change. "Entropy" is what physicists call that process: The equalization of all energy potentials, leading to total immobility. Its social equivalent is the reduction of incomes, living habits, wishes and ideas to a common denominator—the strangling of creative differences, decisions, ambitions.

Thoroughgoing egalitarianism is social entropy. Change demands, and leads to, differentiation and tension. Few among us would want to put a stop to creative change. But more than a few seem to be unwilling to pay the price, in terms of inequality, that change demands.

꿍

Property

SQUARELY across the path of equality lies property. Private property is the classical symbol of economic inequality. Fundamental attacks upon inequality have traditionally taken the form of attacks on property. The defense of property has served, in large measure, as a justification also of economic inequality in a broader sense.

I shall argue that this roadblock today is assuming the form of a red herring. Property is not what it used to be. It is no

longer the main source of inequality of income. Nor is it
limited in total amount, as it was when land represented the
principal form of income-producing property. This takes
some of the edge off the question of why some people happen
to own property and others do not.

The issue of property has agitated society since the dawn
of civilization. Property never has ceased to be under attack.
History is full of movements to share the other fellow's
wealth, since the days when Solon annulled the debts of the
Atheneans and when the Jewish Jubilee Year brought relief
to debtors every fifty years. In response, immense ingenuity
and effort have been called forth to organize property's defenses—legal, political and intellectual. Our attention here
must focus upon the intellectual side of the battle.

Natural law naturally has been invoked on behalf of private
property, as for so many other institutions whose justification
is not immediately obvious. Strenuous efforts have been made
to elevate property rights to the level of human rights—to a
par with freedom and equality. But somehow property rights
have never quite succeeded in establishing themselves at this
lofty height. Perhaps they were held back by the weakness
of the case, or perhaps by an uneasiness on the part of the
sponsors that could conceivably be explained even without
recourse to the Freudian interpretation of wealth. Conse-
quently, the Declaration of Independence speaks of the pursuit of happiness, instead of the pursuit of property.

John Locke, to whom we are indebted for so much of our
political philosophy, sought to strengthen the natural law
argument by relating a man's property to his labor. Property,
Locke said, is imbued with a man's labor, and hence must be
looked upon as an extension of his personality. As such, it
presumably is entitled to the same protection as the owner's

person. Locke displayed remarkable ingenuity in bringing all forms of property under the wing of his protecting philosophy—including land and inherited wealth. Yet it takes a strong self-interest in the conclusion to accept his argument more than halfway. And the argument has always had greater appeal to the rising commercial interests, whose intellectual champion Locke has remained to this day, than to the receding feudal aristocracy with their absentee land holdings.

A more functional note is struck by the view that property must be protected if a man is to enjoy the fruits of his labor. We may be of different minds as to a man's moral right to these fruits—the internal revenue authorities plainly take a dim view of them. But it is in society's own interest to protect whatever a man does manage to accumulate, lest he stop accumulating altogether.

Again, it has been said that property is good and right insofar as it is actively used by its owner. The artisan working with his tools, even the factory owner managing his complex enterprise, score well under this doctrine. Out in the cold remain only the absentee coupon clippers and—logically—the widows and orphans living on a modest competence. Even R. H. Tawney, author of *The Acquisitive Society* and decidedly no friend of private property, saw some good in this sort of distinction.[3]

The historic defenses of property ring hollow in a good many spots. But the charges that have been flung against them likewise are more notable for lofty sentiment than for solid reasoning. Whether it be Proudhon's flat assertion that "property is theft," Veblen's sarcastic pronouncement that property started out as the proceeds of successful raids among primitive tribes and has retained its predatory character ever since, or Marx's ponderous demonstration that property arises from exploitation—these charges will convince chiefly those who already believe. They provide no compelling reason why property should be owned by "the people" instead of by the individual. Nor have the critics told us why, if private property is bad, the people of India should think it good and right that "the people" of France, the United States, or Russia should own and withhold from them the great wealth of their respective countries. Socialist thinking traditionally ends at home.

Certainly the last harsh word on the subject has not yet been said. But meanwhile the subject's evolution, as sometimes happens, has outdistanced the commentators. The complexion of property has changed.

To begin with, as I said before, property today is only one among several sources of income inequality. In years gone by, to be sure, to have a high income was almost synonymous with being a man of property. Agricultural land, urban real estate, and commercial wealth were almost the only sources of a superior income. The growth of the managerial class, the professions, and the bureaucracy (to the extent that one can call its pay "above average") has changed that. It has split the rich into the wealthy and the merely well paid. On a rough and ready calculation, less than half of total income inequality today has its roots in property income.

Secondly, property has become open-ended. As long as the bulk of property was represented by land, property was a closed corporation. X could acquire it only at the expense of Y, and bitterness over who should own a piece of the earth went deep. Today, man-made property far exceeds that made by nature. Potential capital accumulation knows no ceiling, and my gain no longer has to be my neighbor's loss. A great broadening of property ownership bears witness to this de-

velopment. On such terms, the demand for sharing or social-
izing the wealth loses much of its persuasiveness.

Nor have these remained the only changes in the nature of
property. Once conceived of chiefly in terms of productive
wealth, property today has branched out in the direction of
consumers' property. Owner-occupied homes and durable
consumer goods make up a goodly share of total wealth—
homes alone account for $325 billion. And since more than
half of our families are home owners, the have-nots, perhaps
for the first time in history, have in this area become a minority.

Finally, property has changed by becoming less tangible
and less absolute. A man's home may still be his castle, but
the bulk of his wealth is likely to consist of rights and claims
—to receive interest, to participate in profits, to share in the
earning power of an enterprise. These ring less solid than real
estate, and they are becoming increasingly tenuous, thanks
to regulation, union pressure, and the watchful eye of public
opinion. Propertied men may still think of themselves as men
of substance, but their property is becoming progressively less
substantial.

Trends such as these—the diminished role of property in
income distribution, the increasingly open-ended character
of man-made wealth, the growth of consumer assets, and the
progressive sublimation of property—have taken much of the
sting out of the argument. The defenders of property need
no longer snatch at propositions that at times must have
seemed an insult to the intelligence of their audience or a re-
flection on their own. The critics may take such oblique com-
fort as they can from the fact that in the United States they
never stood a chance anyway. In the ensuing calm, both sides
may proceed to reexamine private property on the basis, not

of its rights and wrongs, but of its functional pros and cons.

The functional virtues of private property run parallel, in many respects, to those of private enterprise, discussed in Part II. The two, though not inseparable, always have maintained a close relationship. Hitler and Mussolini for a while succeeded in operating a system that combined private property with a minimum of private enterprise. That combination, however, seems to have been regarded as unstable even by its beneficiaries. The reverse system—private enterprise without private property—so far appears to have looked impractical even to the most arbitrary of dictators.

Private property, therefore, may be said to backstop the role of free enterprise. I had argued earlier that the chief virtue of a free economy is not its productivity but the support it gives to freedom. A dictatorial productivist economy may progress more rapidly in its own peculiar direction. But the impulse must come from compulsion. The chief virtue of a free economy, and implicitly of private property, is the protection it offers against the kind of government which would exert that kind of compulsion.

Private property accomplishes some further decentralization of its own. Power follows property, as has well been said. Property well distributed erects further defenses against concentrations of power, public or private. The caveat "well distributed" is a sizeable one, of course. In the past, property has often been more conspicuous for its concentration than for its dispersion. The public and the government then have both had to be on their guard against the "malefactors of great wealth." But even a small degree of dispersion protects against the kind of power concentration that would come from total government ownership of the means of production.

Private property lends another assist to private enterprise, by providing a powerful incentive. A high income may appear to be all the incentive there need be, for those who remember that "you can't take it with you." But the prestige, power, opportunity, security and further growth of income that come from property must not be underrated. And least of all should we overlook the incentive value of providing for one's family.

Here we come face to face with one of property's darker sides. Property earned has much in its favor. Property inherited is something very different. Yet to be meaningful, property must be capable of being passed on. In this new guise of inherited wealth it leaves many question marks. As an incentive, inherited property plainly works in reverse. William K. Vanderbilt may have gone a little far when he said that inherited wealth did to ambition what cocaine did to morality. But it probably does take an exceptional personality to resist the devitalizing effects of inheritance. And the rotation of society—from shirtsleeves to shirtsleeves—does not happen in three generations often enough to prevent inheritance from creating class distinctions and special privileges, and generally to keep certain people from thinking that they are worth money because they have it. The hereditary rich can argue with some plausibility that money does not make people happy. But the proposition would be more convincing if it were not employed quite so energetically to defend the continued possession of wealth.

The difficulties that hereditary property puts in the way of equality of opportunity we shall consider in more detail presently. For the time being it suffices to have drawn attention to one aspect of private property that is difficult to reconcile with some of our beliefs and values: its hereditary character.

Yet, the productive resources of the nation exist and must be administered somehow. The socialists once tried to per-

suade us that they knew a better way. Government ownership, they claimed, would do away with the difficulties posed
by private ownership. In addition, it would provide new
blessings of its own. Government ownership would remove
inequalities of income; it would raise mass living standards by
dividing up the incomes of the rich; it would humanize relations between management and labor; and it would inspire
the worker with a new enthusiasm once he realized that he
and not the boss was the true owner.

Such modest experience of socialized industry (noted in
Part II) as Great Britain, France and other European countries
have supplied does little to bear out these claims. Inequalities
of income have not disappeared in socialized industries. The
men who reach the upper echelons of these industries do not
appear to be fundamentally different—unless they are political
appointees—from those who advance under private ownership. Their liking for high salaries and perquisites is no less,
their taste for equality no greater, than that of private man-
agers.

Nor has the absence of dividends produced any large surplus available for higher wages. All that can be divided up
among the workers without falling below the rate of capital
formation prevailing under private ownership is the amount
that the owners would have consumed. The sad capitalistic
truth has been revealed that not only can't you take it with
you—you can't even eat it all up down here. And it has been
found not to matter greatly to the workers whether it is the
capitalist or the state who is holding down wages in the interest of capital formation.

The more intimate bond between management and men
likewise has proved something of a mirage. A large organization nationalized is still a large organization. Discipline and

impersonality are as inevitable as before. If the government in power is a labor government, perhaps the management might be more accommodating on wage demands. But of this the workers can have no assurance; meanwhile, the potentialities of a strike suddenly take on a dimmer cast when it has to be directed against the government.

Hope for more enthusiastic performance of nationalized workers, finally, has proved most elusive of all. It is remarkable that this notion could take hold at all in Anglo-Saxon countries, where the idea of working for the government does not generally conjure up a vision of intense labor. The belief that men would work harder for the government would have seemed more appropriate to Karl Marx with his Prussian background. But honest idealists like Tawney made the idea of the dedicated worker an important part of their argumentation. When the British steel industry was about to be nationalized, enthusiastic laborites attributed a sudden upsurge in output to the anticipatory joy of the workers.

Subsequent experience seems to have been disillusioning. The essential point proved to be not who owned the plant, but who did not—in either case, the workers. "Mine is better than ours," said Benjamin Franklin. "Ours is better than theirs," has been the notion of the socialists, but nationalization seems sadly to have failed to shake the workers' suspicion that the organization is, not "ours," but "theirs."

This short taste of socialism can hardly have been conclusive. Yet it has left its mark on socialist programs in many countries. Public control and equalization continue to hold the spotlight. Nationalization is fading into the background. The problem of private property, once a central concern, has lost its sting.

Equality of Opportunity

FOR the better part of this section, equality has remained at odds with goals like progress or freedom. One
species of equality, however, is not involved in this conflict:
equality of opportunity. Capitalism thrives on equality of opportunity. The economy is bound to perform better where
jobs are assigned by the merit system—to each according to
his capacity—and not by nepotism—to each according to his
uncle. Here, for once, equality is on the same team with all
the other virtues.

Their common ground is rather narrow, however, and
scarcely allows room for unlimited rejoicing. Equality of opportunity is certainly no panacea for all the ills bequeathed
by inequality in other respects. Moreover, it would be harder
to organize in practice than some of its admirers seem to think.
This we shall presently see.

Equality of opportunity must be called a narrow virtue
primarily because it seems to envisage human existence as a
kind of race. Only if we all have the same goal—to excel, to
be successful—does it make sense to demand an even start. In
a world where everything is competition and competition is
everything, starting position matters—starting inequality is
inequity. But inequality ceases to be inequity as soon as we
envisage different people following different tracks. The very
term "equal opportunity" loses its meaning once we remind
ourselves that people may have very different goals. How can

we truly equalize Jones' opportunity to live a quiet life close to his family with Smith's to devote himself to intellectual pursuits and Robinson's to make a million dollars?

As Henry Oliver has observed, opportunity in its broadest sense really means opportunity to lead "the good life."[5] This takes different forms for different men. Each wants to start as close to his objective as he can, and it should be of no great concern to him where travelers with other destinations take off from. In other words, where goals differ, what we seek is optimum rather than equal opportunity.

No unfairness need be involved in providing each man with the best start possible toward his particular dream. So long as that dream is to beat somebody else to it, a better start for Jones of course means a worse one for Smith. But Robinson need not be handicapped by arrangements to help Smith become a scholar, if his own ambition remains to become a millionaire. Where competition does not enter in, equality likewise has no function.

If opportunity in this broadest sense is to be maximized, our need is, not for equality, but for freedom. Freedom, first of all, for each to discover what he really wants, free not only from state direction but also from social pressure bent on imposing some homogenized pattern of compulsory felicity. This opportunity to live the good life is something we can all give to ourselves and to each other. If we have not made full use of it, the fault belongs to us and not to our free institutions.

Yet there is no gainsaying the fact that the goals of most of us, in many respects, are competitive. Even where we do not specifically try to get ahead of each other in some particular way of life, we often compete implicitly for economic resources. Smith's scholarly bent calls for expensive libraries and laboratories, the bills for which will in part have to be footed by Jones and Robinson. These two, in turn, will find themselves at considerable odds with each other, over their respective objectives of the thirty-hour week and the million dollars. Some compromise between the interests of the three will always have to be sought.

More than this, however, many of us do, in fact, have very similar goals. We therefore compete with each other in a quite direct sense. America contains a highly emulative society, and emulation immediately splits different into better and worse. A good part of American life does proceed as a race, and each man's starting point becomes a passionate concern to every other. The need for equal opportunity, therefore, still stands.

To make sure, however, that opportunity will knock equally often and equally loudly on every man's door is by no means easy. To do it in a literal way, in fact, is not only undesirable but fortunately also quite impossible. To begin with, it would seem obvious that we cannot mean literally equal job and career opportunities for everybody regardless of aptitude. That would lead to some very witless arrangements. Everybody would have to have the same education stuffed down his throat. To make sure that it was really the same, it would have to be of a pretty mediocre grade. There is not enough first-rate education to go around, and of course it would never do to let one boy go to a backwoods college and another to a distinguished university. Perhaps, to be entirely fair to the under-talented, their abler competitors ought to be subjected to some sort of handicap. Only in that way could we make sure that really *everybody* could be president.

Obviously, no sane society would in this way deprive itself of the services of its most talented members nor deprive those members of the best possible education. Equal opportunity cannot sensibly be interpreted to require equal mediocrity. If what is wanted is the best use of talent, equal opportunity must mean equal chance for equal talent. This, however, would mean very unequal education for the gifted and the less gifted.

On the other side of the fence, equality of opportunity of this more efficient kind is not very helpful if it leads to extreme inequality of results. Darwinian competition of the fit against the less fit may well have that outcome. To argue that this is "natural" does not mean that it is good, nor even that it will be allowed to go on very long. It is always the big boys who want to play the rough games. But they must remember that it is the little fellows who have the votes. They must play the game to suit the majority, or the majority will change the rules to suit themselves.

This implies that people of average ability must have some chance of doing well, and reasonable assurance against doing very badly. Equal opportunity without evidence that the odds are acceptable means very little—as we noted in Part III. It may just mean equal lack of opportunity for the great majority. And of course some floor must be fitted under the "also-rans"—a minimum reward to the unsuccessful—that makes it worth their while to go to the starting post.

But even after all these conditions have been met, the day of the right kind of equality of opportunity is not yet, and perhaps never will be. Suppose we have succeeded in sending the right boys and girls to college and have protected the bright against having to fidget through slow class hours with the dull. Suppose also that we have protected those for whom opportunity knocks in vain against being pushed completely to the wall by those who know how to grab it. Perfect equality of opportunity remains beyond reach so long as we do not abolish the family system.

The family, because it reaches beyond the individual, produces one inevitable effect: it polarizes opportunity potentials. To eliminate the unequal effect of the home upon children's development and education, the state would have to take them into its fatherly arms practically as soon as they learned to speak. To keep fathers from using their influence on behalf of their sons when they start their careers, it might prove necessary to destroy all means of family identification at an early age. That we would have to get rid of inheritance, with all this would mean for the willingness to save and for the continuation of our business system, is just a minor incidental. For, in fact, we would have to turn our society inside out.

Such are the conditions that would carry equality of opportunity to its logical absurdity. Common sense tells us that something acceptable can be achieved on less exacting terms. The United States has long regarded itself as the country of opportunity. Do we offer it on terms of equality that deserve to be called acceptable?

Able men in the United States cannot complain that a ceiling is placed on their future by any system of rigid class barriers. Nor will any really talented youngster have difficulty in getting as much free education, up to any level, as he wants. In other words, in the United States it is true that "you can't keep a good man down."

But what about the others? Here, indeed, we encounter all the invidious distinctions that wealth and background can create. The habit of providing a good education, and the means to finance it; good speech and the right tone; business connections and inherited money—they smooth the path toward good jobs and careers for those who were fortunate in the selection of their parents. Their lack pushes those who were less fortunate toward the routine jobs which our economy rewards with the going wage rate. The moderately gifted son of an Ivy League graduate goes to his father's college and from there to a job for moderately talented Ivy League graduates. The moderately gifted son of a working man goes to high school and thence to the factory.

But this lack of equal opportunity for the less talented is not all. Racial discrimination is a blemish that, in the areas that it blights, works even greater injustice and waste of human ability. The United States deserves no particular blame for being saddled with a problem that most countries have never known. But our failure to solve it hangs like an albatross around our necks. Until this sin is expiated, we can never feel very sure of what we assert about equality of opportunity in our country.

Yet as we contemplate these beams in our eye, we may claim some redeeming features. One characteristic that takes some of the sting out of inequality of opportunity is the rotation in the upper brackets. "From shirtsleeves to shirtsleeves in three generations" is perhaps overly optimistic—if the victims of the process will pardon the adjective. Nevertheless, there is something to the observation that the upper income brackets more often resemble a hotel than an ancestral home. For high salaries, the application is obvious. Property incomes have shown greater staying power. But even here, the tax collector together with the growth of families make the ultimate outcome predictable in most cases. Inequality of opportunity is hereditary only to a limited degree.

A second redeeming feature of the existing inequality can be found in the insidious influence, noted earlier, that it often has upon its supposed beneficiaries. The sheltered life does not usually build muscle and character, nor does it sharpen incentives. Good manners are drilled in, the free use of elbows drilled out, a sensitive conscience instilled, and generally "the native hue of enterprise" undermined. One need weep no tears over the "poor little rich boy" to accept this process as one of the versions of the shirtsleeves to shirtsleeves doctrine.

To sum up our impression on equality of opportunity in the United States: American society has managed to provide equal opportunity wherever it was to the interests of the economy. Able men from all ranks have been pushed ahead by the system, and have found few obstacles in their way. Top jobs thus have generally gone to top men. But we have fewer occasions to pat ourselves on the back when we look at the way the less critical jobs are assigned to the less high-powered citizens. Job performance may matter less in these lower echelons, but the number of lives affected runs far higher. A great deal of work remains to be done here.

V

IN CONCLUSION

As we approach the end of this intellectual journey, it is natural to ask how well the principles we have reexamined are likely to wear in the future. I have argued earlier that the only abiding constant in our economy has been change. We cannot hope to perpetuate both outward form and inner substance. If we want to preserve the dynamic, creative character of our society—and that is the substance of the matter—we must continually break with its old forms. The principles of a free economy have had to adapt themselves to many such changes. The capitalism of today has moved away from the patterns of thirty years ago, and much farther from those of the nineteenth century, adapting its basic principles but never abandoning them. I see no reason why these same principles cannot absorb the changes that surely lie ahead.

The essence of the principles that have passed reexamination in this book can be put in very few words. First, it seems implicit in the way we conduct our affairs that we value a free economy mainly for its service to freedom, political as well as economic, and only secondarily for its productive prowess, impressive as that has been. If our concern were primarily with maximum production at whatever cost, a forced draft economy of the type employed in two world wars would probably commend itself to us, as it does to the communist world. Second, we have considered the incentives demanded by a competitive economy that depends upon many centers of decision. Finally, we have noted how, in an economy so organized, it becomes necessary to accept a certain amount of economic inequality, which will nevertheless make all its members better off in the end than they are likely to become under a more egalitarian system.

In one word, we have seen that, in a material sense, freedom comes at a cost, not at a profit. These alternatives of greater or lesser freedom, of weaker or stronger incentives, of tolerating more or less economic inequality, will continue to be with us even though the form of our economy changes substantially. In the course of normal evolution, or perhaps under the compulsion of greater urgencies, we may find ourselves shifting the signposts that today mark our position on these issues. Yet as long as alternatives exist, there is room, and a need, for the old values.

To try to foresee the particular problems that may test these values in the future is an interesting but dubious exercise. History has not been kind to prophets. To demonstrate the inevitability of an event after it occurs has usually proved easier than to diagnose its probability before, and even the clearest vistas vouchsafed by the crystal ball have often faded. In particular, problems that expert opinion has concluded to be permanent and insoluble have shown a remarkable tendency to disappear soon thereafter. That has been the fate of such celebrated propositions as the "new era" of permanent prosperity in the 1920's, the "mature economy" of the 1930's, the "inevitable post-war depression," and the "permanent dollar shortage" of the late 1940's and early 1950's. Perhaps the doctrine of inevitable inflation that had gained ground recently may in time be added to the list. Some of these predictions may have been self-defeating because people believed them. Some may have disturbed us sufficiently to produce corrective action. But the value of the prophecies has suffered rapidly diminishing returns as the future turned out to be rather different, if no less troublesome, than anticipated.

Instead of speculating on the future, it seems more practical to focus on two contemporary issues and on the proposals that we are receiving for handling them: (1) The "growth" issue—that we should urgently accelerate the growth of the economy, and (2) the "fewer gadgets, more services" issue— that we spend too much on tailfins and TV's, too little on education and other public services.

What position can rationally be taken on such propositions by those in sympathy with the ideas of this book?

⁊⁊⁊

More Growth

THANKS to the invention of the national income accounts, everybody can and apparently almost everybody does now watch economic growth play by play. The enthusiasm over the discovery of "growth" would almost make one suspect that in our grandparents' day there had never been such a thing as "progress." The new visibility of growth has endowed proposals to accelerate growth with drama and appeal. International competitive comparison lends a sense of urgency.

This atmosphere has brought into flower a range of proposals to accelerate economic growth. Some would involve methods that are in keeping with the principles of a free market economy. Others call for easy money and deficits even at times of high activity. Some aim at important needs and uses. Some seem to come down to little more than a numbers game played to keep up with the Russians or to impress a gallery of uncommitted countries. Some proposals seem heavily burdened with the mortgage of self-interest.

Later on I shall have to take issue with some of the more questionable of these proposals. But in no case would I want to be counted among those who would deny growth a high priority. Growth is important. The ways of attaining faster growth demand the best thought of all of us. That needs to be said first of all.

One arrives at this belief not without some hesitation. It is by no means a foregone conclusion. We are already much the richest country in the world. If there is anything that ails us, surely it is not a lack of material goods. As we become still richer year after year, the importance to us of further additions to income should diminish, not increase. We may well feel tempted to ask whether we do not sidetrack the cultural and moral growth of the nation with an overemphasis on purely material gains. Undoubtedly there are jobs to be done, goals to be reached, evils to be mended. We have the resources to do it. But could we not treat them as particular jobs, assign the necessary resources, and get them done? Must we stir ourselves into a frenzy of growth, trying to accelerate everything across the board in order to meet these selected needs? Isn't the sensible way to reallocate some of our existing resources, cut some less urgent expenditures, expand the more urgent? If people sincerely feel that tailfins and TV's should have lower priority than defense and education, why can't we shift from one to the other until our priorities are in better balance?

We have done this from time to time in the past—when the pressures became sufficiently strong. The nation has never hesitated, in wartime, to limit its consumption in order to provide the resources for victory. In peacetime, too, we have accepted tax burdens far beyond the worst fears of most of us. The full financial impact has been brought home to us of the old Chinese malediction "may you live in interesting times."

But in a free society, there are limits to this process. These limits shift slowly if at all in the absence of emergency. The balance of forces that determines the division of resources between private and public use, and between different uses in each of the two sectors, proceeds from many powerful pressures. It is not readily dislodged by a small number of articulate advocates. These advocates do not all pull in the same direction —some want more of this, some of that—they neutralize each other. A large part of the tax-paying population believes that the proper direction for taxes to move (if not the most frequent) is down, not up. These taxpayers do not react kindly when told by the advocates of bigger public spending that they are simply asking for a handout like so many others, and are apt to observe that it is their own money for which they are asking. From such conflicting forces, a balance emerges capable of considerable stability. It is this balance created by the many that impedes the ready provisioning of needs thought urgent by the few.

I would certainly not argue that major reallocations of resources should not be welcomed or could not be accommodated by the economy if the citizens want to make them, although perhaps not without some clashing of gears. Nor am I saying that the democratic process will under no conditions make such a shift. But I think it is clear that massive shifts of resources are not easily decided upon. With the two political parties on the whole very close to each other ideologically, with consumption habits firmly embedded and aggressively promoted, dramatic events or a very well supported leadership would be needed to make us revise at all drastically our gentle habits of money spending.

If this diagnosis holds, the consequence is painfully clear—a substantial advance in any one form of expenditure pre-supposes an advance in all. We shall have to expand all around, allowing everything to stay more or less in proportion. More public expenditures presuppose more private. If more is to be spent on education or defense, we must also accept— many of us with little enthusiasm—more tailfins and TV's. The first condition of doing any particular public job, on this diagnosis, is an expansion of the revenue base. The first condition of peoples' raising any major item in their private budgets is to raise their expenditures as a whole, though of course not in equal proportions. To suppose otherwise seems to conflict with a well established balance of wants—or with the freedom of the taxpayer and consumer to maintain that balance. So long as that freedom is not to be overridden, our society probably will use it for ends that seem lacking in a sense of urgency and national purpose. Once more we come up against the fact that freedom has its price.

This, it seems to me, is the strongest argument for urging rapid growth upon even a wealthy society. The general need for greater resources is small. But particular needs do have pressing present claims. If we do not want to take care of these by tightening our belts elsewhere, we must do so by adding some fat all around. By the same reasoning, if we are unwilling to accelerate all-round growth, we must resign ourselves to seeing our particular priorities met more gradu-ally. Urgencies that could be accommodated only if growth were to proceed by forced draft methods are seen to have a very high cost.

One other concern about growth stands out in the context of this book. I have argued that a free economy, depending as it does upon strong incentives, must accept economic inequality. To those who have succeeded in getting on the right side of inequality, many good reasons will occur that justify this condition. To the considerable majority who have not, the only argument likely to carry appeal is that the resulting more rapid growth will benefit them more than would redistribution coupled with slower growth. Inequality of shares implies a commitment to accomplish betterment through growth.

This commitment has generally been well met. That is one of the principal reasons why our society has not been plagued greatly by demands for redistribution of income or wealth and other manifestations of class struggle. Such tendencies will remain more soundly dormant the better the commitment can be met hereafter. By the same token the pressures for higher wages, which we have strongly felt, can be absorbed more easily without inflation. Economic growth is the key to many perplexities that would become oppressive without it.

This much said on behalf of the importance of growth, some caveats are now in order. For some of the growth enthusiasts, economic growth has become something like an escape from economics itself. Economics traditionally has been billed as dealing with the allocation of *limited* resources to alternative ends. Those who put their growth models through their paces before our astonished eyes seem to demonstrate that we can have more of everything at the same time— if only we grow faster. With scarcity gone, do we still need economics?

It is an illusion, of course, to think that we can ever meet all our needs, growth or no growth. The trick is performed by establishing supposed "needs" at a level a little beyond our reach, and demonstrating that 1 or 2 per cent added growth would bring them within reach. We have no basis for supposing that at a higher level of available resources, competition among alternative uses would be much less severe. It would still be as painfully true as it is now that a little more of this means a little less of that. The resources available to us today for all purposes surely would have seemed immense twenty years ago. They appear barely adequate now. The resources that growth may yield twenty years from now may seem to exceed our present concept of "needs." I doubt that we shall find it so when the time comes. Growth is not likely to repeal economics.

The role that growth can play in solving our international problems likewise falls well short of a panacea. It is by no means self-evident that differences in Gross National Product determine relative military posture. Willingness and ability to concentrate resources for a particular purpose are at least as important. Neither is it evident or even plausible that the percentage gains scored by our economy will determine the decision of the uncommitted countries to adopt one or the other of the rival systems. Insofar as economic considerations and examples are decisive at all, the performance of European economies, which also are in a phase of "catching up," is likely to speak more eloquently. In short, there is little to show that the issues between us and the rest of the world will be governed predominantly by our economic successes, or that we can buy safe survival with an additional per cent or two of economic growth.

These are strictures to be made of excessive claims on

behalf of the problem-solving power of economic growth. They are needed to supply perspective. But the principal issue to be raised with the growth enthusiasts must be, not over the merits of growth in general, but over their particular purposes and methods. When we look at these schemes, it becomes readily apparent that some of them have little to do with promoting growth. Economic growth has simply become an attractive new label to paste on an old package of big deficit spending and easy money proposals. General government expenditures, whether supported by honest idealism or selfish interests, do not necessarily accomplish much in the way of economic growth. Welfare expenditures are right and good in their place, but a good part of them is pure consumption. Expenditures benefiting particular interests or sectors of the economy frequently are of little general value; quite often they are harmful. Those who label these as "growth expenditures" are trading on a confusion between growth in capacity, which is the essence of economic growth, and a more intensive straining in the rate of use of existing capacity. Greater expenditures of this sort may push the economy closer to the limits of its capacity. But they do so at the serious risk of damaging it in the process, through inflation for instance. They do not increase its capacity, and so fail to produce growth in this more basic sense.

The proponents often claim, to be sure, that rising demand will stimulate rising investment and thereby raise capacity and generate true growth. What they do not observe is that what we consume we cannot invest. If more resources are devoted to consumption, less will be left over for investment. That is as true of public spending for consumption purposes as it is of wage increases that go at the expense of investible resources. To say that at times the economy has some idle

resources of labor and materials in reserve, and that by em-
ploying these we can have more consumption and more investment at the same time, is a superficial approach. The fuller
use of these idle resources, when they do exist, is of course
desirable. But that is strictly a one-shot operation. When the
economy functions at reasonably full capacity, the alternative
of more consumption or more investment cannot be avoided.
We cannot grow faster by consuming more.

The ploughing back of a high share of output into investment is an essential condition of growth. That is brought
home to us every day—by the countries that are investing
much and growing fast, and by those who are investing little
and not growing much. The belief that one can have more
growth through more consumption is not shared by the
countries that are doing a good job of growing.

Among those who today project ambitious growth plans,
there are many, of course, who recognize the need for investment. They allow for it in their plans—often with a strong
accent on public investment, including such intangible but
probably effective forms as education. What many such
schemes have in common with those urging principally more
consumption is a tendency to overwork the economy. They
tend to strain its resources and capacity beyond the possibility
of balance, by trying to do too much at once. Put into effect,
such schemes would create demands exceeding supplies.
They would set too much money chasing too few goods.
Prices would rise, scarcities would develop, and the economy
would become disorderly. That situation does not commend
itself as a firm basis for further growth.

Those who would strain the economy to the utmost limits
of its physical capacity are disregarding, in effect, the restraints
imposed by free markets and by finance. This disregard has

had its forerunners in our economic history, though under very different conditions. During the Great Depression, some people who called themselves technocrats had a similar view of the economy. They saw it as a piece of machinery whose only function was to produce, without regard to problems of selling and financing. This engineer's view of economics was, in effect, the technocrats' answer to the problem of insufficient demand that harassed us during the recession. Their present-day successors are proposing to accord the same treatment, albeit at a more sophisticated level, to what would be a condition of insufficient supply. They are arguing, in effect, that all that can be produced can be financed and distributed without bottlenecks and imbalances. Only production counts; the financial and the market functions of the economy are taken for granted.

The phrase "what can be produced can be financed" has a familiar ring to economists. It comes from the days of World War II. It was very largely true then. Finance was—rightly—not allowed to be a limitation on output, even though the government had grossly to inflate the money supply to pay its bills. The financial consequences—strong inflationary pressures—were blocked by price control. The market consequences—severe shortages and imbalances—were suppressed by consumer rationing and by controls over materials and manpower. Freed from the need to maintain financial and market equilibrium, but fettered in every other sense, the economy was able to turn out vast amounts of the products the government demanded.

A vision of that kind of economy is not acceptable to us in peacetime. Yet I suspect that in order to accommodate the more extreme growth plans, something along those lines—though more moderate—is what we would have to do. If we were prepared to restrict the consumer, control prices, wages, materials and manpower, and if nothing counted but an increase in output—with the government as the principal customer—we might generate growth enough to outgrow the Russians. Our economy would also have become so like theirs, however, that the meaning of the competition would have vanished.

This unpleasant vision conforms to an observation made earlier. I ventured to conclude that a centrally controlled economy run with ruthless disregard of the consumer could show more rapid growth than a free economy. I also concluded that only a dictatorship could conduct such an economic policy. A centrally controlled economy responsive to consumer wishes and operated by a democratic government would run a grave risk of getting the worst of both worlds— the free-wheeling consumption and relatively low savings of the free economy, and the loss of individual initiative and the frictions of an over-governed central system. This, precisely, is the dilemma that the growth extremists must face. To do it with tight controls is effective but unthinkable. To try it without is quite thinkable but probably not effective.

This of course is hardly the last word that can be said about growth. If dictatorial methods are alien to us, if the overextended welfare state seems unpromising, we still do not need to leave future growth entirely to the free market—unless we so desire. The free market has done very well by us. But the free market is not primarily a device to procure growth. It is a device to secure the most efficient use of resources. How much growth results in the process depends upon how much of the output is saved and ploughed back into investment. A free market could function with perfect efficiency and yet show very little growth, if the participants chose to consume all its output. A conscious decision is open to us, therefore: How much we want to reinvest in growth. This is a choice that each consumer and each business man must make for himself. But we can supplement those decisions by the political processes of democracy.

The degree to which we can improve upon the performance of the free market by the methods of a free society must not be overrated. Growth in the past has been remarkably stable, leaving out of count the temporary ups and downs of wars and the business cycle. It has averaged about 3 per cent since 1909, about 3½ per cent since World War II. Within the latter period, it proceeded somewhat faster during the earlier years that included the Korean War, and somewhat more slowly during the later years which included the demobilization. A recent study by a Congressional committee estimated that in highly favorable conditions, including virtual absence of recessions, but without forced draft methods, the growth to which we might look forward over the next fifteen years could amount to 4.5 per cent. Under much less favorable conditions, including fairly frequent interruptions of growth, we could expect 3.4 per cent. This range is consistent with a more general appraisal given in the President's *Economic Report* for 1960. As far as the scope of possibilities is concerned, there hardly seems to be much left to argue over.

The list of actions open to us for sustainable growth contains no trick devices. Avoidance of recessions ranks high. The loss of investment during those periods, more than the loss of production, slows down growth over the years. Avoidance of inflation is likewise important. Though in the short run inflation may act as a shot-in-the-arm, in the long run it is bound to disorganize the economy and lead to trouble—perhaps to controls that we want to avoid. Improvement of the tax system would help, although the amount of help that tax reform can give to growth probably is much overrated.

A good-sized budget surplus at times of high activity would aid growth materially. It would tend to reduce consumption while making more resources available for investment. It would allow an easier credit policy without risk of inflation. Freer markets, stimulation of competition, and greater consequent efficiency would help. Opportunities for appropriate action both in the private and the public sphere are not lacking. Strong incentives, enlarged educational opportunities, and intensified research are other major aspects of growth. Each of them has played an important role in the past, and remains capable of future contributions. Public expenditures of many kinds are helpful in their time and place. They must, however, remain within the limits of available resources and subject to the conscientious exclusion of special-interest expenditures masquerading as growth oriented. Maintenance of an adequate work week, finally, and a halt in the present rapid trend toward ever shorter working time, deserves a high place on the list of actions directed toward growth. We are not likely to grow faster by working less.

These are the principal actions that a free society can reasonably take to accelerate its economic growth. Their result should be sufficient under most conditions. Situations could be envisioned in which they might not. Should we have to meet such conditions, we should go into them with a clear realization that greater economic performance is likely to be achieved only at a serious sacrifice of freedom.

ᴄᴘ∙ᴏ

Too Many Trivia?

IN ADDITION to free advice about growth, the nation has received helpful suggestions of another sort, in a rather opposite vein. It has been argued that we have all the production we need and to spare, but that too much of our growth has gone into private consumption, too little into public. We are said to be wasting our substance on trivia while allowing urgent public needs to go uncared for. This view does not complain of inadequate growth. But it sees us riding in tail-finned, oversized automobiles through cities that are becoming slums, finds our children sitting glued to the latest TV models but lacking schools where they can learn to read properly, and generally charges us with putting private profligacy ahead of public provision.

The general doctrine that in the United States public needs tend to be underfinanced in relation to private I first heard many years ago from my old teacher Alvin Hansen. It has always seemed to me to possess a measure of appeal. Throughout this book, I have been at pains to argue that with rising wealth and industrialized living, the need for public services advances, and probably faster than living standards. In part this reflects simply the familiar fact that the demand for services tends to expand faster than the demand for goods. In part, the social conditions of modern life are also accountable for the growing need for government services. Private business is learning to meet many of these new needs—for instance in the field of insurance. It is not inconceivable that some day we shall become rich enough to be able to indulge increasingly a preference for privately supplied services. But at present, and as far ahead as one can see, the trend seems the other way. I would footnote this reference to my earlier passages by observing that to recognize a rising trend in the need for public services and to claim that at present we have too little of them, are two different things. The more than doubling of federal and also of state and local expenditures since 1950 should drive home that distinction.

The thesis that public services are neglected and private consumption inflated with trivia has found its most eloquent interpretation in *The Affluent Society* by John Kenneth Galbraith,[1] to whom we were previously indebted for important insights into the workings of American capitalism. Galbraith argues that this imbalance is nourished by advertising, which creates artificial wants. He sees it further accentuated by an obsession with production, which keeps us from realizing that our problems are not those of want, but of affluence. The imbalance is epitomized by our supposed tendency to limit public expenditures to what is strictly essential, while we apply no such criterion to private expenditures.

One may reasonably argue that Galbraith exaggerates the distorting influence of advertising. That would not alter the basic assumption on which his thesis rests—the assumption that there are better wants and worse wants. Scientific detachment notwithstanding, I find it extraordinarily difficult to disagree with this proposition. To rate an attendance at the opera and a visit to an (inexpensive) nightclub as equivalents, because the market puts a similar price on them, goes against my grain. So does the equation of a dollar's worth of education and a dollar's worth of chromium on an automobile. And a plausible case could probably be made, on the basis of the evolution of the species, that opera and education do represent more advanced forms of consumption.

But what consequences, if any, should be drawn from such judgment? Does it yield a basis for trying to discourage the growth of the less "good" expenditures? In a free society, we obviously want to move with the utmost circumspection. It is worth remembering that even Thorstein Veblen, who went to some extreme in deriding the "leisure class" and its "conspicuous consumption," did not take an altogether negative view of all conspicuous waste. In *The Theory of the Leisure Class* he said, "No class of society, not even the most abjectly poor, foregoes all customary conspicuous consumption. . . . There is no class and no country that has yielded so abjectly before the pressure of physical want as to deny themselves all gratification of this higher or spiritual need."[2]

For a fair appraisal of the case against trivia, we would also want to know the approximate size of the bill that is being incurred for various frills and frivolities. Gadgets in cars and homes have drawn the special ire of the critics. It is interesting to note, therefore, that expenditures for all kinds of durable consumer goods, including automobiles, run about 14 per cent of personal consumption. The greater part of this, presumably, goes for the essential parts of fairly essential equipment. What is left for ornaments and gadgets does not loom impressively large.

Whatever our private feelings about the gadgetry in our life, we probably do well not to stress them too hard. It is only too easy for some members of a community to work themselves into a fit of righteousness and to feel tempted to help the rest regulate their existence. In an extreme form, and not very long ago, this happened in the United States with the introduction of prohibition. Some of us may lean toward special taxation of luxuries, but surely no one wants sumptuary legislation banishing from our show windows and homes the offending contrivances. A new puritanism directed against wasteful consumption, however understandable, would make no great contribution to an economy that requires incentive goods to activate competition and free markets. Neither would it be compatible with the freedom that we value.

It is the positive side of the case—the asserted need for more public services—that must chiefly concern us. One can listen with some sympathy to the case and to the account of the biases in our economy that work against public and for private spending. The pressure of $10 billions worth of advertising is a bias of that sort. The natural reluctance of taxpayers to vote taxes the benefits of which will be shared by others is a second. A third is the somewhat vague nature of many public benefits—education, welfare, and health, for instance. They are of a kind that the taxpayer himself might tend to neglect a little were he to purchase them in the market place. Then there is the peculiar relationship of state and local authorities to the federal government, which restrains public expenditures by leaving most of the socially useful expenditures to the former while giving the more productive tax sources to the latter. And finally, there is the American tradition which in the interests of freedom puts a special premium on private activity over public.

But what we are in some danger of overlooking are the biases on the other side—the pressures that work for greater public spending. If advertising promotes sales to individuals, those who supply the public authorities are not without means of their own to promote their wares. If some taxpayers object to taxes that will benefit others besides themselves, there are others who vote for expenditures expecting that they will benefit where they have not contributed. Politicians in general have not been averse to voting funds for well supported worthy causes. Vocal minorities that know what they want often can outmaneuver inarticulate majorities that don't know how to stand up for their own interests. Finally, our tax system itself has a built-in bias to encourage spending, because it collects relatively small amounts per head from taxpayers in the lower brackets, while those in the upper brackets pay a good deal. If the benefits that individuals in different brackets derive from public services are not too disparate, taxpayers in the lower brackets obviously are getting theirs at a bargain. Since they constitute a majority, they are in a position to increase the number of these bargains.

As between the forces that inhibit and those that advance public expenditures, no one can say for sure where the balance lies. But on the evidence that thirty years ago taxes of all kinds added up to less than 10 per cent of the Gross National Product, whereas today they account for well over 25 per cent, we have no reason to suspect that the expansive forces lack vigor—even allowing one-third of the present load for major national security.

Meanwhile, those who would like to see public services taking a still larger share must bear in mind two facts, one economic, the other political. The economic fact is that the free provision of public services paid for by taxation is a very inefficient way of catering to consumer needs. I am not referring to popular suspicions about the efficiency of public administration, but to the manner in which costs and benefits are adjusted to each other, or fail to be adjusted. In private dealings, the consumer purchases the exact amount of the exact product he wants, and so gets the most for his money. The taxpayer voting for certain public services has no means of securing such nice adjustment. He may find himself getting less, or more, or something other than he wanted. He has no incentive, moreover, to economize in the use of many of the services offered—usually they come to him free of charge. Our methods of making public decisions and apportioning public services leave much to be desired as compared with the neat job done by the free market.

The political problem that confronts advocates of larger public expenditures is of a different order. We return here to the point stressed earlier in this section—the tendency of our society to produce a balance of interests that impedes ready shifts among private and public resources. This applies also, of course, to budgetary expenditures. Barring some outward disturbance that shakes the balance of interests, such as a military emergency, the balance of expenditures in the budget will also tend to remain stable. If there are to be budget cuts, they are likely to cut all around. If the purse strings are to be relaxed, they are likely to be relaxed not just in one direction, but in all. That is the result of a balance which makes all interests share burdens and benefits in accordance with their bargaining strength.

The consequences, when larger expenditures are proposed, tend to be those we have often observed. The proponents of new expenditures rarely demand that all forms of public spending be enlarged. They have some particular purposes in mind. But the prevailing balance of interests works against such favors for any one group, extended to the exclusion of all the rest. If one form of expenditures is expanded, political pressures develop for giving everybody else something he wants.

The "balance of interests" effect need not, of course, be taken in its most literal sense. Obviously the proportions among different public expenditures always are shifting in some degree. Some expenditures are subject to factors that cannot be controlled, such as fluctuating interest rates or crop yields. Some have a built-in momentum, as does Social Security. And as public opinion and political constellations shift, so does the balance among public functions. Marginal improvements in particular public programs are never out of reach. Major increases, however, are not likely to occur unless accompanied by major shifts in the balance of interests. With that balance intact, the politics of the case incline toward, not "first come, first served," but "come one, come all."

This imposes a heavy surcharge upon expenditures that intrinsically may have much to recommend them. It alters the practical attractiveness of such proposals. To spend public money for a good program is one thing. To have to loosen up on half a dozen unrelated programs as a condition of expanding one is quite another.

A political surcharge of this kind can make the implicit cost of desirable programs very high. Some may argue that this cost will have to be faced. Nevertheless, it should give pause even to those who feel strongly about their proposals. In a free country, no group can expect to change the balance of interests save as they succeed in swinging some of its components to their side. Once more we must note that freedom has its price.

* * *

In the appraisal of a need for faster growth, for more public services, freedom usually appears on the side of the scales that weighs against the quickest way of attaining a goal. It has been the contention of this book that we must make our peace with that fact. We do not know what the future may bring. It may well hold urgencies and periods that would make the fact more difficult to live with. But we should also remember that long-run forces work on the side of freedom. In the long run, as wealth grows, some of our wants and needs will gain strength relative to the rest. Freedom is one of these. As our material needs are more fully met, the value of freedom will stand out with ever increasing clarity. We should find ourselves increasingly willing to pay its price.

NOTES

II

[1] Karl Mannheim, *Freedom, Power and Democratic Planning*, (London, Routledge and Kegan Paul Ltd., 1951), p. 15.

[2] David E. Lilienthal, *Big Business: a New Era*, (New York, Harper & Brothers, 1952); Adolf A. Berle, Jr., *The 20th Century Capitalist Revolution* (New York, Harcourt, Brace and Co., 1954).

[3] Friedrich A. Hayek, *The Road to Serfdom*, (Chicago, University of Chicago Press, Phoenix Books, 1956 ed.), p. 48.

[4] Hayek, *op. cit.*, p. xiv.

[5] Edwin G. Nourse, *The Nineteen Fifties Come First*, (New York, Henry Holt and Company, 1951).

[6] John Kenneth Galbraith, *American Capitalism: The Concept of Countervailing Power*, (Boston, Houghton-Mifflin Company, 1952).

III

[1] Arnold J. Toynbee, *A Study of History*, abridgement by D. C. Somervell (New York and London, Oxford University Press, 1947).

[2] Joseph A. Schumpeter, *The Theory of Economic Develop-*

ment (Cambridge, Mass., Harvard University Press, 1949; German edition, 1911).

IV

[1] Board of Governors of the Federal Reserve System, *Federal Reserve Bulletin*, July 1959, p. 713.

[2] Simon Kuznets, *Shares of Upper Income Groups in Income and Savings* (New York, National Bureau of Economic Research, 1953); Simon Kuznets, "Economic Growth and Income Inequality," *American Economic Review*, March 1955.

[3] R. H. Tawney, *The Acquisitive Society* (New York, Harcourt, Brace and Company, Harvest Books edition).

[4] Tawney, *op, cit.*, pp. 147 ff.

[5] Henry M. Oliver, Jr., *A Critique of Socioeconomic Goals* (Bloomington, Indiana University Press, 1954), p. 61.

V

[1] John Kenneth Galbraith, *The Affluent Society* (Boston, Houghton-Mifflin Company, 1958).

[2] Thorstein Veblen, *The Theory of the Leisure Class* (New York, The New American Library, 1953), p. 70.

Index